GROWING
THROUGH
MID-LIFE
CRISES

Contents

Preface

When was the last time you heard a sermon on Ecclesiastes? Most preachers (including myself) tend to skip this somewhat depressing portion of Scripture and preach on something more positive and uplifting. But while working on a class in "adulthood and aging" for my Ph.D. in psychology, I noticed that many of the authors were saying the same things about the mid-life transition that Solomon had said so emphatically years before.

I decided to preach a series of sermons on the Book of Ecclesiastes. (After all, the word *Ecclesiastes* is translated "The Preacher.") The combination of these sermons, my research, and my *own* mid-life crisis produced this book.

No one knows for sure that Solomon wrote the Book of Ecclesiastes; but he surely *might* have. If he did, he probably wrote it during or after his own mid-life. James Draper, author of *Ecclesiastes: The Life Without God,* asserts, "Most scholars believe that David's son, Solomon, wrote this book" (p. 8). On the other hand, G. L. Archer, writing in *The Zondervan Pictoral Encyclopedia of the Bible,* vol. 2, states, "The Solomonic authorship of the book is regarded by most modern authorities as purely fictional" (p. 184). Note that they both claim to associate with "most" scholars or authorities. They can't both be right.

This book assumes that Solomon *was* the author. From that assumption comes this point: *The things that people strive for—power, wealth, fame—do not satisfy. Solomon knew. He had them.*

A word about names of persons. Unless they are public figures, the names are purely fictional. The stories, though changed enough to protect the persons involved, are true.

Another word, this about the many quotes in the book. I decided to list in alphabetical order all the *substantial* sources (and a few other helpful books on mid-living)—and do so in the back of the book rather than footnoting each reference. This makes a cleaner text and still helps guide further reading if you desire. Minor quotes are referenced in the text only.

I believe that Solomon has a lot to teach us about life, mid or otherwise. This book is about that time from 35 to 55 when so many of us seem to reevaluate our lives and which so many of us experience as a crisis. If you are in this age group—approaching it or still suffering from the effects of it—listen to "the Preacher."

I
The Problem

All the world's a stage,
And all the men and women merely players.
They have their exits and their entrances;
And one man in his time plays many parts,
His acts being seven ages. At first the infant,
Mewling and puking in the nurse's arms.
And then the whining schoolboy, with his sachel
And shining morning face, creeping like snail
Unwillingly to school. And then the lover,
Sighing like furnace, with a woeful ballad
Made to his mistress' eyebrow. Then a soldier,
Full of strange oaths, and bearded like the bard,
Jealous in honor, sudden and quick in quarrel,
Seeking the bubble reputation
Even in the cannon's mouth. And then the justice,
In fair round belly with good capon lin'd,
With eyes severe, and beard of formal cut,
Full of wise saws and modern instances;
And so he plays his part. The sixth age shifts
Into the lean and slipper'd pantaloon,
With spectacles on nose and pouch on side,
His youthful hose, well sav'd, a world too wide
For his shrunk shank; and his big manly voice,
Turning again toward childish treble, pipes
And whistles in his sound. Last scene of all,
That ends this strange eventful history,
Is second childishness, and mere oblivion,
Sans teeth, sans eyes, sans taste, sans everything.
                —William Shakespeare, As You Like It, *Act II,*
            Scene 7

1
What's It All About?

Everything is meaningless.
— Solomon

Mark looked tired. Not just your basic I've-had-a-hard-day-at-the-office-let-me-rest-a-minute tired, but more of an I-don't-know-if-I'll-ever-move-again-or-if-I'll-ever-want-to sort of tired.

He slumped in my chair, staring at the wall with the look of the man in the television commercial who has not yet taken the Dristan. "I just don't know what I'm gonna do," he sighed. "Nothing excites me anymore. Oh, I go through the motions. I get to the office on time, answer my phone calls, play some golf, go to church; but I don't really care about any of it."

Mark was a handsome, well-dressed man of about 50 who had been urged (nay, driven) to see me by his very worried wife and grown son. He had worked hard all of his life trying to be worthy, trying to provide "all the things I never got from my father."

He became a vice-president in his company, an elder in his church, and president of his service club. He had been active in politics, a devoted (though often absent) father, and an excellent golfer and skier. He vacationed in Paris, Geneva, and St. Croix. He was being urged to run for city council. He was considering suicide.

Your Basic Mid-Life Crisis

Mark was depressed. Recently, he had lost all interest in sex—both with his wife of 30 years *and* with his girlfriend of the past year-and-a-half. The affair, Mark's first, had begun with a shout and was ending with a whimper. "She doesn't understand my lack of desire . . . and neither do I."

Emma, Mark's wife, was enduring his lack of libido with her characteristic sarcasm. "The last time we had any excitement in bed," she chortled, "was when the electric blanket developed a short circuit."

Sex was not the only activity in which Mark had lost interest. He had lost 15 pounds because "the sight of food turns me off." He had stopped playing golf or attending church regularly. And he had begun goofing off on the job. "Oh, I can get away with it for a while," he said, "but, sooner or later, it'll catch up with me. Someone upstairs will notice that my assistant has been writing all my reports and that I've stopped paying attention in staff meetings. I haven't come up with a new idea in almost a year . . . and I don't care."

Mark's therapy had begun with a shout, like his affair. His wife had discovered the girlfriend ("It was just too much work to hide it anymore") and had walked out. The shock temporarily stimulated Mark, and we began a flurry of activities, one of which was our therapy. Recently, however, as with most depressed people, the sessions, too, were slowing down to a whimper.

Therapy was hard for Mark. He had grown up with heroes like John Wayne, Humphrey Bogart, and Gary Cooper. Strong, silent men who had everything under control. Their women adored them; their enemies feared them; their friends respected them. They didn't *have* problems; they *solved* them. Expressing tenderness, fear, or sadness was for their womenfolk. Crises were solved with strong words, quick decisive actions, guns, or fists. Psychotherapy was for the weak, the sick, and the crazy.

Our sessions had begun to degenerate into a predictable pattern. Mark would walk slowly into the office, look about suspiciously, take off his suitcoat, and place it on my desk chair. He would then lean back in a reclining chair and sigh deeply. After a few minutes of silence he would take out a cigarette, look at it, then glower at me. (I do not allow smoking in my office.) "Well, now what?" he would say.

Mark believed in the "fixer" system. Take your problem to someone with the right tools. Given enough time, money, and talent, *he* fixes it. But in psychotherapy, the person with the problem enters into an intimate relationship with a therapist in order to uncover lost feelings, wishes, dreams, and such so that the client can end up fixing the problem himself. This was beyond Mark. The fact that he didn't really believe in the psychological system complicated our time together even more. Mark had invested his time and money; he was beginning seriously to doubt my talent.

But Mark did believe in the Bible (though he had not read it much). Since I do, too, this gave us a point of common reference. We discussed themes of grace ("Could God forgive him for cheating on his wife?"), justice ("Why should *he* have these depressive feelings after trying so hard to be a good Christian?"), and love ("Was it what he felt for his wife, his kids, or his ex-girlfriend?").

The Light Dawns

Somewhere during our third or fourth month together, Mark began to read the Scriptures with a passion. He also read an article on the mid-life crisis. "This sounds a lot like me," he said.

"It is you."

"Maybe, but how do I reconcile this hopelessness with the message of the Bible?"

In one of those rare fits of intuitive brilliance which come to every therapist occasionally, I remarked, "Haven't you ever read Ecclesiastes?"

"No."

"Well, *read* it. I think Solomon was depressed just like you—and for no apparent reason. He seemed to have it all, and he didn't care, either. Try it. Maybe it'll help you to understand yourself."

Mark did read Ecclesiastes, and it did help. He saw Solomon struggle with the meaning of success, money, pleasure, religion, love, and wisdom. He read about Solomon's fear of death, his bitterness at giving all his hard-earned wealth to his sons, and his sadness that no one would remember him. It struck a chord somewhere in Mark's soul. It fit.

I wish I could say that Mark made miraculous progress, that his depression left immediately, and that he and Emma lived happily ever after. That's what I would *like* to say. What I am *able* to report is that Mark began to make small bits of progress, that his depression slowly began to subside, and that he and Emma began to put a new relationship together with fear and trembling.

Mark was not a unique case. Calling the time between 35 and 40 the "deadline decade," writer Gail Sheehy claims that most people experience an "authenticity crisis" during that time. All of a sudden they begin to ask questions that never occurred to them before.

"I'm halfway to the grave. What have I done with my life? What am I going to do with the rest of it? What do I really believe in? Look at that body in the mirror, that flab, those wrinkles, that gray. Is that *really* me? Do I want to be stuck with the same old routine, boring job, nagging spouse, demanding kids? Is there a way out?"

One of the myths of childhood promises that "when we grow up, we can be whatever we want to be." We dream of becoming a pro football quarterback, counterspy, the president of the United States, or at least a doctor, lawyer, or vice-president of a company. Then one day we wake up to find that we are almost 40 and will never do anything great. The "impossible dream" is just that—impossible.

Mike Yaconelli says it this way:

Mid-life crisis occurs ... when, as in Robert Rains' book, *Success Is a Moving Target,* you wake up one morning to find that the target you've been aiming for all of your life has moved. . . . Apparently, many of us who call ourselves evangelical assume that mid-life problems happen to other people, people who don't have Jesus in their lives. . . . If we believe this, we are wrong. (*The Wittenburg Door*)

Take, for instance, Charlie Harris. Charlie spent the first 25 years of his life flunking out of a number of schools, taking drugs, getting in trouble with the law, and "generally trying hard *not* to be the kind of son my parents expected." To this end, he found himself drifting from job to low-paying job, getting "thrown out of the Marine Corps on my ear," and being divorced by his first wife.

Then, at age 25, something happened to Charlie. As he tells it, "I was sort of like the prodigal son, sitting in the mud and eating with the pigs. All at once I realized that there had to be something better than this. I stopped trying to tear down the image that my parents had created for me and straightened out my life."

Charlie made peace with his surprised parents, started attending church (where he experienced "a profound sense of salvation and peace with God through Christ"), went back to night school, married a nice girl, and started selling insurance. He was on his way.

"In the insurance game," said Charlie, "no one cares what you *used* to do or what kind of jerk you were. The only thing that matters is, 'How much are you selling *now*?'" The job gave Charlie a fresh start, and he took full advantage of it.

Charlie rose quickly from salesman to group leader to district manager. He won pins, rings, vacations to the Bahamas. He moved his family about the country about once every four years. Judy, his second wife, was at first thrilled, then disappointed, then depressed with the moves. Charlie was never home. His son and two daughters saw little of him.

When I saw Charlie, he wanted me to placate his wife, who had filed for a divorce. He was now 42 and due to move to another state. Judy had put her foot down. "You move to Kansas City *alone!*"

"Talk some sense into her," he stormed. "You gotta make her see it, Doc. God says that women are supposed to be submissive and follow their men and support them. The Bible is against divorce, and you've got to make her see that she's wrong."

Judy, however, was adamant. "He's been pulling that submissive bit for 17 years," she said evenly, "and I'm through buying it. I've fixed up two apartments and four homes and left them. The kids go crazy every time we move—and for what? So that he can work 24 hours a day, seven days a week, pulling together another failing district, and get another plaque on the wall?"

Charlie, trying to deal with *Judy's* mid-life crisis, turned down the new job and resolved to spend more time at home. When I saw him again two years later, Judy's depression had resolved, but *his* was in full bloom.

"Doc, the last time I came to see you, it was to get my wife back. This time it's for me. I'm scared, Doc. I don't know what's wrong with me. I've lost interest in my work, and my sales are off 16 percent. I listen to a song on the radio or see a show on TV and start to cry. I try to talk to my wife and kids, but they're too busy. I feel sad and nervous at the same time. I pace the floor. I eat too much, and I've started to drink again. I've stopped going to church at all, but, strangely enough, I feel closer to God than ever. And I know I pray more. What's wrong with me?"

Charlie, too, was helped a great deal by reading Solomon's account of the mid-life crisis. Just knowing that a famous Bible hero went through the same problem seemed to make Charlie's problem easier to bear. "I can't be *too* stupid," quipped Charlie, "if someone as wise as Solomon had these same thoughts."

A The Mid-Life Crisis Is Not Only for Men

At age 35, the average mother sends her last child off to school. If, like many women, she has been trained by her culture to exist only to care for others, what does she do now? Have another child? Drink herself into oblivion? Go back to school?

Watch continuing daytime dramas? Bother her children or grandchildren to death?

Regina, 39, mother of four, a high school dropout, was ready to drop out of her family. She was referred to me by her mother, who said Regina was "going crazy." Regina agreed. She stated in our first interview that she had "absolutely no reason to act this way." One day she would yell at everybody for no apparent reason, and the next day she would cry and feel guilty about it.

Regina, the oldest of five children, had been the family babysitter. Raised by an alcoholic mother and a passive father, Regina's unhappy childhood was filled with demands for more work, with abuse from her mother and neglect by Dad. "My brothers and sisters were my only source of love," she reminisced, "but I bitterly resented them, too, because I had to take care of them all the time."

When Regina was 16, she met Bruce. He was 21; he had a job and a car. Mom and Dad disapproved of Bruce. By age 17, Regina was pregnant and married. She had gotten away from the enslavement of her parents' home to find a new one of her own making. She spent every waking hour of her new life trying to please Bruce and her ever-increasing brood.

But Bruce never seemed to be happy, in spite of Regina's efforts. And so, finally, after the last child was safely sent off to school, she became a high school graduate, then a registered nurse.

Regina threw herself into her work with a passion. When that didn't satisfy her, she threw herself into an affair with an even greater passion. For a while it looked as if the family would disintegrate. Then, after the affair cooled (they almost always do), Regina began to come out of the crisis. She is stronger now. She likes herself better—and so does her family (after a bit of readjustment). "Oh, Bruce hasn't changed," she admits. "Probably never will. But I seem to be able to accept him now and love him for what he is instead of screaming for him to be someone else."

Bruce has changed one thing, though. He accepts Regina for who *she* is. "I've demanded that and gotten it," Regina says. "If I hadn't, I don't think I would have stayed."

Judy, Mark, and Charlie (and their respective families) were caught up in a phenomenon that I now believe is almost universal to American culture. It may not be experienced as a crisis, and it may not occur exactly at mid-life. But it *will* occur to most of us at *some* time, whether as a long series of small doubts or as one big one.

Poet and musician Mason Williams repeats his mid-life question 15 times in a row: "What's it all about?" Twenty-two times he answers, "I don't know" (*The Mason Williams Reading Matter*).

F. Scott Fitzgerald described his experience at 39 as

> a feeling that I was standing at twilight on a deserted range, with an empty rifle in my hands and the targets down. No problem set—simply a silence with only the sound of my own breathing. (*The Crackup*)

Solomon (at age 55?) looked back on his mid-life crisis and described it to us:

> I, the Teacher, was king over Israel in Jerusalem. I devoted myself to study and to explore by wisdom all that is done under heaven (Eccl. 1:12-13a).

And what did this wise teacher find?

> What a heavy burden God has laid on men! I have seen all the things that are done under the sun; all of them are meaningless, a chasing after the wind (1:13b-14).

Surviving the Crisis

*L*ike Fitzgerald, Solomon wrote down his mid-life fears, his anger, despair, and disgust. Unlike Fitzgerald, however, who came to the conclusion that "the natural state of the sentient adult is a qualified unhappiness," Solomon advises us to

> go, eat your food with gladness, and drink your wine with a joyful heart . . . . Fear God and keep his commandments, for this is the whole duty of man (9:7a; 12:13b).

Why do Fitzgerald and Solomon, both famous and wealthy writers, start with the same premise (that life had gone sour) and come up with such different conclusions? Fitzgerald drank himself into a fatal heart attack at the age of 44. Solomon "imparted knowledge to the people. He pondered and searched out and set in order many proverbs. The Teacher searched to find just the right words, and what he wrote was upright and true" (12:9b-10).

I propose that the difference between these two great writers is Solomon's deep, underlying faith that God is in control of the universe. "I know that everything God does will endure forever; nothing can be added to it and nothing taken from it" (3:14a). It matters greatly to whom great questions are addressed. Fitzgerald questioned himself about the meaning of life and found no answer; Solomon questioned God. Therein lies the difference.

2
Healthy, Wealthy, and Wise . . . and Depressed

Oh, life is a toil, and love is a trial;
Beauty will fade and riches will flee.
Pleasures, they dwindle, and prices, they double;
And nothing is as I would wish it to be.
            —Anonymous Folk Song

Solomon, unlike David, his father, or Saul, the first king over
Israel, was a city boy. He was cosmopolitan, well educated, and
used to being rich. Jerusalem, the "City of David," had begun
to be the center of the nation's power, wealth, and culture. The
Israelites, under Saul and David, had advanced from a group
of tent-dwelling shepherds, living under constant fear of attack
from their Philistine, Moabite, and Egyptian neighbors, to a
major power in the Middle East. Former enemies now paid
tribute; trade had been started; and buildings were going up.

Solomon, as befitted the son of a king, was used to the
best—the choicest food, the most stimulating conversation from

world-traveled teachers, excellent physical training, and a thorough education in the books of Hebrew law.

More importantly, Solomon was also tutored by his father. David was a sensitive poet and a deeply spiritual man. He advised his son, "When one rules over men in righteousness, when he rules in the fear of God, he is like the light of morning at sunrise on a cloudless morning, like the brightness after rain that brings the grass from the earth" (2 Sam. 23:3b-4).

One can almost hear David groan with shame as he writes the next verse: "Although my house be not so with God" (v. 5a KJV). David realized that he had blown some marvelous opportunities for personal growth and for establishing his kingdom's trust in God. David's majesty is that he knew it. He looked into himself with a fearlessness unknown to most men, and seeing himself naked before God, he repented. David was, therefore, able to conclude in this section of Scripture that God "hath made with me an everlasting covenant, ordered in all things, and sure" (v. 5b KJV). Solomon, thus, received from David a legacy of wisdom and spiritual insight along with the riches and power. He had known a father who had walked with God.

Too Much of a Good Thing?

Solomon, because of his cosmopolitan upbringing, was also politically astute. Solomon's very birth was clouded in intrigue. His mother's first husband, Uriah the Hittite, was murdered by David's command so that he would not know that Bathsheba was pregnant with David's child. Though the child died, Bathsheba's second son, Solomon, was David's favorite. It was expected that Solomon eventually would become king, even though several of his half-brothers (by David's other wives) had prior claim to the throne by virtue of their age. Solomon was well aware that he was not exactly beloved by his relatives and had seen several of them die in political struggle. Absalom, the most infamous, actually had led a somewhat successful revolt against David for a time. Solomon had seen trusted officials leave his father's side when the going got rough. He also knew that popular opinion is fickle, based upon "what have you done for us lately?"

Solomon knew how to maneuver in these unsure waters. When it looked like his half-brother Adonijah would assume the throne, Nathan the prophet and Solomon's mother, Bathsheba, intervened for him with David. With their help and the help of Zadok the priest and Benaiah, a trusted army official, Solomon won the day (1 Kings 1).

As soon as Solomon had firmly established himself with the people, he proceeded to eliminate the opposition coalition. He had Adonijah and Joab (Adonijah's military support) put to death. He banished Abiathar the priest. He then had Shimei, an old adversary of his father, killed for a minor infraction.

But in acquiring all this political savvy, Solomon seems to have lost something of the very essence of his father: David's almost innocent simplicity. David may have made some gross errors in judgment—indeed, some very sinful errors. But people always knew where he stood. He was emotional and sometimes illogical. He could be a shrewd politician also. But when he made a decision, he usually asked simply, "What do You want, God?" and then obeyed. David was, at the core, "a man after [God's] own heart" (1 Sam. 13:14) and, therefore, was greatly beloved by his people.

Solomon was respected, looked up to, even revered by Israel—but he never won their love as David had. His political maneuverings were at once his triumph and his downfall. He instigated a number of marriages to foreign women that were designed to stabilize his position in the Middle East and to increase trade. He succeeded. He also succumbed to their idolatry, made altars to Chemosh and Molech, and "turned away from the Lord" (1 Kings 11:9).

But if Solomon ended rather badly, his beginnings were grand. "Solomon showed his love for the Lord by walking according to the statutes of his father David . . ." (1 Kings 3:3). And one night as he lay sleeping, God spoke to Solomon in a dream and said, "Ask what you want from Me, and I will give it to you." Solomon replied, "Give me wisdom and an understanding heart so that I can judge your people." Then God said, "Because you have asked for this, you will be wiser than anyone has ever been or will ever be. Not only that, but I will give you great riches and honor, even though you didn't ask for them" (1 Kings 3, my paraphrase).

God's Promise of Wisdom

> God gave Solomon wisdom and very great insight, and a breadth of understanding as measureless as the sand on the seashore. Solomon's wisdom was greater than the wisdom of all the men of the East, and greater than all the wisdom of Egypt. He was wiser than any other man ... (1 Kings 4:29-31a).

I suppose everyone has heard about the two prostitutes who wanted Solomon to judge which of them was the mother of a disputed baby (1 Kings 3:16-27). That a king would spend time with "petty" (i.e., nongovernmental) problems illustrates Solomon's "breadth of understanding" of people's hurts. His solution (to saw the child in half, thus stirring the chords of motherhood in the woman who said, "No, don't do that; let *her* have him") attests to his great wisdom.

Solomon's wisdom gave Israel the only time in its history, from Moses to the present, that it was *ever* considered a great world power. Solomon was wise politically, militarily, and economically. He built an empire that has never been equalled by Israel to this day. He alone of all the kings was able to keep peace in the Middle East. His trade agreements were economic strokes of genius.

By keeping peace, Solomon was able to divert great sums of money toward building projects, not the least of which was his own palace. The greatest of all, however, and the nearest to his heart, was the building that became known as "Solomon's Temple." The temple took 180,000 workmen and 3,300 supervisors seven-and-a-half years to build. Aside from the salaries, which are not given in the Bible (at today's union wages, the temple would have cost over 260 billion dollars), the temple had over a half-billion dollars in gold and silver used as building materials. (See 1 Kings 5—7.)

God's Promise of Riches

One can see from the above that Solomon had come a long way from the tents of Saul and David. Aside from the temple, Solomon's personal yearly income has been estimated at over 127 million dollars. "All of the king's dishes were made of gold; silver was not considered important enough in the days of Solomon" (1 Kings 10:21 Goodspeed). Plus he had the financial ability to support 700 wives and 300 concubines *and* their hundreds of children. (Sandals alone must have run him a small fortune!)

God's Promise of Honor

> He was wiser than any other man . . . . And his fame spread to all the surrounding nations. He spoke three thousand proverbs and his songs numbered a thousand and five (1 Kings 4:31-32).

The queen of Sheba heard of Solomon's fame and decided to visit him. She was impressed. After she had inspected the buildings and had listened to his wisdom, she exclaimed: "They told me you were really something, but they didn't tell me the half of it! I didn't believe it till I saw it with my own eyes. Your wisdom and prosperity far exceed anything they told me" (1 Kings 10:1-7, my paraphrase).

> King Solomon was greater in riches and wisdom than all the other kings of the earth. The whole world sought audience with Solomon to hear the wisdom God had put in his heart (1 Kings 10:23-24).

So, what's my point? Just this: If I, John Sterner, tell you that money, power, education, wisdom, and fame aren't all there is to life, that by themselves they don't satisfy, that they go flat and taste stale after awhile; you have the perfect right to say, "How would *you* know, John?" But if *Solomon* says "it's all vanity, emptiness, chasing after the wind," maybe you'll take him seriously.

Solomon had it *all*.

> I became greater by far than anyone in Jerusalem before me. . . . I denied myself nothing my eyes desired . . . . Yet when I surveyed all that my hands had done . . . everything was meaningless, a chasing after the wind; nothing was gained under the sun. . . . So I hated life . . . (Eccl.2:9-11, 17).

Solomon had it all—wine, women, and a mid-life crisis: "My heart began to despair over all my toilsome labor under the sun" (2:20).

Not everyone has a mid-life crisis, and not everyone who *does* has it at 40. Maybe you didn't have one; or maybe you won't. Chances are, you know somebody who will. Or is. Or did. So give the book to them. But first read it yourself. It will help you understand them better. (And, besides, you never know . . .)

3

The Big Four-Zero

As fish are caught in a cruel net,
or birds are taken in a snare,
so men are trapped by evil times
that fall unexpectedly upon them.
— *Solomon (Eccl. 9:12)*

On Tuesday, October 19, 1982, John Zachary DeLorean was arrested, charged with conspiring to deal 220 pounds of cocaine, and thrust into the news. He was 57. This "golden boy" of the auto industry, who had earned over a half million dollars per year while working for General Moters, was in handcuffs.

DeLorean was "a different person" to those who knew him in his earlier years. They described him as a man of outstanding ability, personal charm, and drive. He had a photographic mind, remembering even page numbers of articles he quoted. He was a natural leader in school and soon rose to the top in business. The son of a Detroit factory worker, he was named a group vice-president of GM, in charge of all domestic car and truck divisions.

But something happened to the young head of Pontiac Motors on the way up.

He turned 40.

"He became a flamboyant character after he discovered California [at age 40]," says a friend. "He went for a whole new non-Detroit look." Reconstructive surgery on his face, a new wardrobe, and slightly shaggy hair were the first changes made. He sought out new friends, divorced his wife, and started dating show-business personalities. He remarried, this time to Kelly Harmon, daughter of the Michigan football great, Tom Harmon.

"He was double her age and playing like a sophomore in high school," says an acquaintance. "It was like something out of *Andy Hardy Goes to the Prom.*" Four years later, DeLorean left General Motors.

It is not my intention to either romanticize or demean Mr. DeLorean. He was acquitted by a jury. It *is* my intention to point out that, in my view as a psychotherapist, part of his change was his failure to negotiate successfully his mid-life crisis. You and I have little chance of falling so far—simply because we have little chance of rising so high. Our falls, however, cause just as much pain, just as much sorrow, and just as many unnecessary consequences as that of great men like DeLorean. Or Solomon.

There are hundreds of books and articles about the mid-life crisis. (Many are listed in the back of this one.) I do not intend to present all of the information, nor will I attempt to kid you that I'm the top authority in the field. What follows is distilled from those top authorities and represents the current thinking on the "who, when, what, where, how, and why" of the basic mid-life crisis.

Who: Not Everyone, and Some More Than Others

Some folks (the lucky few) never seem to have a crisis due to age. They grow and develop consistently throughout life, much like an oak tree grows from an acorn. These folks usually grow up in stable homes, marry stable partners, work in stable jobs, and raise stable families. When asked about turning 40 (or 30 or 65), they reply that it's "no big deal; everybody does it."

Isaac, son of Abraham, seems to have been that kind of person. None of the tense, conflict-ridden situations that marked the life of his father and his sons appears to have happened to Isaac. He tended to his sheep, loved his wife, worshiped God, and entered the "hall of faith" as listed in Hebrews 11.

Not that Isaac was a perfect person. He made some poor decisions. But he never seems to have experienced either his faults or the inevitable problems of living as *crises*. He simply accepted his shortcomings and the ups and downs of life and went on. Some people are like that.

A somewhat larger, but less fortunate, number of persons are more like Isaac's son Jacob. He never seems to be *out* of crises, most of which are his own doing, beginning with the winning of his birthright by cheating his brother and (literally) pulling the wool over (under?) his father's eyes. The crises continue through his deceiving and being deceived by his uncle Laban, his attempt to wrestle with an angel, his confrontation with Esau, and his final evaluation of himself: "My years have been few and difficult" (Gen. 47:9).

For some folks *every* developmental change in their life becomes a crisis. These folks typically come from unstable or unloving homes, lead unstable or unloving lives with their families, and get little satisfaction out of life. Age 40 is looked upon as a terrible event; but so was 30, and so will be a number of other ages and events. They are typically stuck in one emotional frame of reference: always angry or afraid or depressed. People rarely ask them how they are doing because they are tired of hearing a current list of illnesses or an angry and bitter evaluation of the world.

David and Moses represent a third example of how persons react to crises. For David the events revolved around adultery, murder, and an attempted cover-up. Moses experienced at least two major crises in his life: the murder of an Egyptian and the subsequent exile to Midian, and an encounter with Jahwe in the burning bush.

Both Moses and David were devastated by their crises. Both were emotionally upset. Listen to the fear of Moses as he pleads with God, "Who am I, that I should go to Pharaoh?" (Ex. 3:11). Read the despair and anguish of David in Psalm 51. But both Moses and David were enriched by their experiences, and both went on to serve God well. Both are mentioned in Hebrews 11, as are Isaac and Jacob. Solomon is conspicuous by his absence.

Solomon illustrates a fourth way people react to crises. As a young man, he seems to have had it all together. He sought wisdom from God, became rich, famous, and powerful, built great buildings, and lived in a grand style. Whatever triggered his crisis is unknown. The nature of the crisis is well told in Ecclesiastes.

The crisis ended in a severe shaking of Solomon's faith. He seems not to have taken his own wise advice to "fear God and keep his commandments" (Eccl. 12:13). Rather, he slides into debauchery and idolatry.

> The Lord became angry with Solomon because his heart had turned away from the Lord . . . . So the Lord said to Solomon, 'Since this is your attitude and you have not kept my covenant and my decrees, which I commanded you, I will most certainly tear the kingdom away from you and give it to one of your subordinates' (1 Kings 11:9a, 11).

S *When: It Can Happen at Any Time*

Some persons, as I mentioned, can have multiple crises at any time and at various times. Some have a big one at age 30 when they no longer feel "young." Some have a crucial time at 65 when they are forced to retire. The *mid-life* crisis, however, is substantially different in origin and meaning from crises at age 30 or 65. It happens from age 35 to 55, but most often at 40. For some persons, it is experienced suddenly.

"I woke up one day and thought, 'What difference does it make if I go to work or go to Bermuda or just stay in bed all day?' " remarked one of my clients. "Of course, I went to work; but the meaning, the pizzazz, was all gone. I looked at all the bosses and secretaries running around like we always did, and I asked myself, 'What's the big deal?' "

For others, like myself, the crisis builds up slowly. My first book, *How to Become Super-Spiritual or Kill Yourself Trying,* was written during a slowly building crescendo toward40, when the crisis peaked. As I reread the book now, I can see the anger and sarcasm directed at the church system, which ultimately became directed at myself (where it belonged). I criticized the church for being inconsistent and phoney, which it frequently is. The criticism, however, was a cover-up defensive maneuver for the *real* problem: *I* felt inconsistent and phoney (which I frequently am).

In my experience, most of those persons who experience mid-life crises in their 50s do so because they have repressed the problem. When it finally hits, it hits with the original force *plus* the force of the released repression. Picture a person gradually compressing a huge spring for 40 years, and then compressing it even more tightly for 10 years more. Once released, the force of years dispels itself in a few short months. The shock can be devastating.

What: Different Things to Different People

Contrary to some popular opinion, there is no correct way to "have" a mid-life crisis. Nonetheless, most of us experience some of the following symptoms, in differing amounts of intensity:

1. A Dread of Aging. At middle age, my body shows signs of change. I am grayer, slower, and have acquired a paunch. My back hurts, I nap more, and my eyes are weaker. I have wrinkles. Two of my kids have flown the nest, and I could be a grandfather in a year. I am getting old.

Levinson, one of the leaders in the field of middle age, writes:

Middle age activated our deepest anxieties about decline and dying. . . . One is no longer young and yet not quite old. . . . Youth is vitality, growth, mastery, the heroic, whereas old connotes vulnerability, withering, ending, the brink of nothingness. . . . It is terrifying to go through middle age in the shadow of death. (*The Seasons of a Man's Life,* pp.ix-x)

Solomon said something similar.

Man's fate is like that of the animals; the same fate awaits them both: As one dies, so dies the other. All have the same breath; man has no advantage over the animal. Everything is meaningless. All go to the same place; all come from dust, and to dust all return (Eccl. 3:19-20).

"The fear of death," writes Irvin Yalom in *Existential Psychotherapy* (p. 27), "plays a major role in our internal experience; it haunts as does nothing else; . . . it is a dark, unsettling presence at the rim of consciousness."

To get rid of this "dark, unsettling presence," we generally suppress our fears; we "try not to think about it." And till midlife, we generally succeed. But death or near-death of close loved ones has a way of ripping through our carefully spun web of self-deceit. Then, instead of rumbling under the surface, death fairly screams at us, "YOU TOO WILL DIE."

Somehow, the old religious answers seem to stick in our throat and taste filthy when death first becomes real. The same Scripture passages that have calmed and soothed us for years begin to make us rage with indignation. Heaven sounds like an empty platitude, and we *know* where the sting of death is.

2. A Loss of Illusions. Some writers use the word *middlescence* to describe the similarity they see between middle age and adolescence. It is worth noting that the two go together; children reach their teens about the same time as parents approach middle age.* The rejection of our established values

---

*Some couples put off *having* children until they are approaching middle age. It will be interesting to see how these couples differ in mid-life from those who start families much younger, since the children born to mid-lifers will not be teens until their parents are in their late 50s.

and institutions by our teens causes us also to reevaluate those values and institutions. Often they are found wanting. James Conway writes:

> It is extremely difficult to live with a man who is going through the mid-life crisis. Some days he may act like an adolescent, with great outbursts of anger, or deep depression, or withdrawal. . . . He doesn't know who he is, where he is going, what he is doing. His values are confused.

"He won't take us to church anymore," Alice spat out crisply and evenly to me. "We never used to miss church. Sunday nights, prayer meetings, special services—we never missed. He taught Sunday school. He was a deacon. Now he just doesn't care. And because of him, now the kids won't go, either."

"I just don't seem to be interested anymore," admitted Hank, Alice's husband. "We tried changing churches. Twice. But, she's right; I just don't care anymore. I know I *should* care. I want to be the spiritual leader, but . . . I don't know what's wrong. How can I make my kids go to church when *I* don't go?"

Hank discovered that his real problem was a lack of faith in God, brought about by a loss of illusions about the church. He had discovered that church people were still people. Their hearts were deceitful and desperately wicked; their tongues were untamed; their salvation depended on grace. Hank eventually learned to forgive the church—after he forgave himself. During the meantime, Alice learned to assume more spiritual leadership and insist that the teens accompany her to church.

3. A Negative Reaction to a Changing Culture. When I was young, I knew what life was about. Bad guys wore little mustaches and black hats. Germany and Japan were enemies; China and Russia were allies. John Wayne always fought for the right and never kissed the girl. Music was sensible. ("Marzie doats and dozie doats"; or was it "Mares eat oats and does eat oats"?) Boys played with balls and guns; girls with dolls and jacks. F.D.R. was regarded as a saint.

Nowadays, *my* music is heard only as nostalgia. Boys wear

earrings, and my daughter wants to grow up to be a cop. F.D.R. is cursed for the mess our system is in. John Wayne was a drunk in one of his last movies. My dentist wears a beard and looks like a kid. Young people live together before marriage and some instead of marriage. Churches sponsor "Christian Punk Rock" concerts. Just when I thought I was ready to play the game of life, somebody went and changed all the rules.

4. A Reevaluation of Life Goals. Sometime between 30 and 40 years of age, I woke up to the fact that I was never going to pastor a large church. I had always depended on part-time work to support myself, in the illusion that someday—someday—I would be a "successful" pastor.

But, slowly, the light began to dawn. I was a successful marriage counselor, an excellent public speaker, and a decent writer. But, as a pastor, I was ineffective. I'm still not sure exactly why I was not effective; but when I finally decided to quit and devote more time to the things I do well, I felt like a great weight had been lifted from my shoulders. I also felt ashamed and guilty for failing God and myself.

Some "successful" persons also change their goals, but for very different reasons. Their success has not satisfied them. Think of the stereotypical executive who leaves the rat race to become a beachcomber. The change often occurs because the man has become more connected to his "feminine" component. He has become less like Alan Ladd and more like Alan Alda. Money, power, and the esteem of others begin to mean less to him than creativity, freedom, and connectedness to others.

While some men become more "feminine" at mid-life, many women get to be more "masculine": more assertive, powerful, and anxious to do something besides raise children and cater to men. Carl Jung, in 1930, was the first to document this phenomenon.

> How often it happens that a man of forty-five or fifty winds up his business, and the wife then dons the trousers and opens up a little shop where he perhaps performs the duties of a handyman. There are many women who only awaken to social responsibility and to social consciousness after their

fortieth year. . . . Very often these changes are accompanied by all sorts of catastrophes in marriage, for it is not hard to imagine what will happen when the husband discovers his tender feelings and the wife her sharpness of mind. ("The Stages of Life," *The Collected Works of Carl Jung* vol. 8, p. 398)

It is hardly coincidental that this "sharpness of mind" comes to the woman at the time when the last of her children are safely tucked away in school. Many of my female clients have gone back to school, found jobs, or gotten involved with socio-political organizations. It's not that parenting is suddenly worthless; it's just that she now has enough time for something else.

5. A Profound Sense of Loneliness. "Pity the man who falls and has no one to help him up" (Eccl. 4:10b). The reality of death can make any one of us believe that we are truly alone in the world. And trying to find someone to talk to about the previous four symptoms will intensify this fifth one. Erich Fromm puts it this way:

> The awareness of his aloneness and separateness, of his helplessness . . . all this makes his separate disunited existence an unbearable prison. The experience of separateness arouses anxiety; it is indeed the source of all anxiety . . . .
> To be separate means to be helpless, unable to grasp the world—things and people—actively; it means that the world can invade me without my ability to react. (*The Art of Living*, p. 7)

Some of the more lonely people I know are pastors. "Every day I provide comfort and understanding for countless people," lamented a pastor-friend-client of mine, "but who listens to *me*? Who knows that *I* hurt, doubt, hate, or lust?" Every day some of these (usually middle-aged) pastors quit and find other jobs. They are no longer willing to tolerate the loneliness.

The rejection felt by mid-lifers in general who question the old values increases the loneliness. Hank (mentioned previously) lost all of his friends when he left his church. "I thought those people *liked* me," he said softly, "but they forgot all about me when I stopped coming to their church. Now I wonder if anybody likes me just for me."

Many women who become more powerful experience loneliness, too. "People don't seem to know what to say to me or how to treat me anymore," said one of my clients recently. "Even my family is more distant somehow—like I have a disease or something."

6. An Ominous Feeling that Life Has No Meaning. "Emptiness, emptiness, says the Speaker, emptiness, all is empty. What does man gain from all his labour and his toil under the sun?" (Eccl. 1:1b NEB).

A recent suicide note read:

> Imagine a happy group of morons . . . carrying bricks in an open field. As soon as they have stacked all the bricks at one end of the field, they proceed to transport them to the opposite end. This continues without stop. . . . One day one of the morons stops long enough to ask himself what he is doing. He wonders what purpose there is in carrying the bricks. And from that instant on he is not quite as content with his occupation as he had been before.
>
> I am that moron . . . . (Anonymous, from *Reflections on the Human Venture*, Cantril & Bunstrad)

This is the *core* of the mid-life crisis and the core of Ecclesiastes. "I have seen all the things that are done under the sun; all of them are meaningless, a chasing after the wind" (1:14). If all is meaningless ("vanity," as the KJV calls it), then what *is* the meaning of life? Irvin Yalom writes,

> The question takes many forms. . . . What is the meaning of *my* life? *Why* do we live? *Why* were we put here? What do we live *for*? What shall we live *by*? If we must die, if nothing endures, then what sense does anything make?(*Existential Psychotherapy*, p. 423)

This is the cry of David, "My God, my God, why have you forsaken me?" (Ps. 22:11); the wail of Job, "Why did I not perish at birth, and die as I came from the womb?" (Job 3:11); the query of Solomon, "What's the use of working so hard?" (Eccl.

2:11, my paraphrase). This is the core of everyman: either life makes sense or it does not. If it does, well and good. But if it *does,* why does it seem *not* to? And if it does *not,* . . . .

For the Christian, Jesus is the answer. This I firmly believe. But Solomon asked the questions.

4

The Big Four-Zero (Continued)

The long, dull, monotonous years of middle-aged prosperity or middle-aged adversity are excellent campaigning weather [for the devil].
—*C. S. Lewis,* Screwtape Letters

So far, we have looked at *who* gets the mid-life crises, *when* it hits, and *what* it is. Now we examine *where* it is likely to happen, *how* it is experienced, and *why* it exists in the first place.

Where: Anyplace; Anytime

Persons in mid-life crisis can be divided roughly into two groups: those who have problems in specific areas, and those who carry the crisis wherever they go. Harry is one of the former.

"I'm fine at the office, Doc, or at social events. But, everytime I hear certain hymns in church, I just want to cry. At home I'm a bear—and God help anyone who crosses me on the expressway."

Violet, on the other hand, is "in the pits everywhere, and all the time. There isn't *anything* that gives me joy or gets me excited. I don't care if the house is clean, if the kids get fed, if I play golf or not, or if Sam is mad at me. It's like I'm in another country or on drugs or something."

The Family—Garbage Dump of the Mid-Life Crisis

For many of those in crisis, the family is *where* it will be acted out. We tend to be able to stifle negative feelings when on the job or in social situations. When we get home, we let it all hang out. The spouse and kids receive both the anger and the dissatisfaction we feel toward them as well as the rage we have stifled in other places. How sad that the people we love the most get the worst part of our personality simply because we believe they will not reject us.

Families with adolescents make up a large part of professional family therapy. Very often the problem lies not so much with the teenager as with one or both of the middle-agers with whom the teen lives. The psycho-sexual traumas of adolescence awaken the forgotten memories of their parents. The parents' anxiety is fed back to the teen who now has *twice* as much trauma as before. The teen explodes, and the battle begins.

Clara, a mother of two teens, had called me because "if I have to endure one more fight with these two, I'll either run away or commit mayhem!" When I asked to see the whole family (as is my usual practice), she doubted that her husband, Sam, would come, and she didn't want to "drag the little ones through this." I insisted that knowledge is power and that Sam and the little ones had some knowledge that no one else had. Clara, Sam, two teens, and two younger children grouped into my office and wondered what I would do next.

After interviewing each member, it became clear that the teens *were* obstinate, obnoxious, and verbally abusive; *but to only one person: Clara.* They were fine in school, in church, and with the other members of the family (at least, as fine as teenagers normally are). Clara, however, was dissatisfied with her children, her husband, and her lot in life. Exit the family; enter individual therapy for Clara based around the near-empty nest syndrome and the mid-life crisis.

Of Course, You Hate It; That's Why It's Called Work

A number of mid-lifers find their primary dissatisfaction with their job. (Of course, as I have pointed out, the housewife's job and family are the same thing.) The job that seemed so necessary, and even exciting, now drags. Many persons switch jobs during mid-life; the story of the executive quitting the rat race to run a chartered boat is the stuff beer commercials are made of.

Some of those stories are true. Gauguin left his bewildered wife and a successful banking career at 35 to become a leading post-impressionist painter by the age of 41. Elliot Jaques, the developmental psychologist who probably coined the phrase "mid-life crisis," was intrigued by Gauguin and other artists, such as Dante, Beethoven, Goethe, Ibsen, and Voltaire, who seemed to experience a profound change in their work in their middle and late 30s.

Jaques examined a random sample of 310 artists, writers, painters, and composers of superior gifts. He discovered the emergence of three different patterns. First, the creative capacity was sometimes expressed in mid-life for the first time, as in the case of Gauguin.

Second, the death rate of these artists shows an alarming jump between the ages of 35 and 39. Artists who died during this time include Mozart, Raphael, and Chopin. The death rate then drops below normal and stabilizes in the late 40s.

Third, the artists who go through mid-life usually show profound changes in their work. Shakespeare wrote his comedies as a young man; his tragedies during his 30s. One can see large differences in the pre and post mid-lives of Dante, Keats, and Shelley. I am persuaded that my own preaching and writing is a lot different (and better) after 40. Happily, this is also the opinion of my wife and colleagues.

Warning: Changing jobs may be a positive result of the mid-life crisis, but it will not avoid the crisis, lessen its intensity, or shorten its duration. It may also make the crisis *worse* if you jump too fast. "I blew 21 years seniority for a job that's just as meaningless as the old one," bemoaned one of my clients.

How: Let Me Count the Ways

*T*here are as many ways to experience the mid-life crisis as there are mid-lifers. Nonetheless, some patterns emerge. I'll briefly list them here and expand on them later.

The person in crisis is responding to some or all of the symptoms listed in chapter 3:

1. Fear of aging and death
2. Loss of youth's illusions
3. Reaction to cultural change
4. Reevaluation of life's goals
5. A sense of being alone in the world
6. Meaninglessness of life

One may respond to these six problems with a shout or a whimper. Those who respond with a shout make good copy. Solomon, Dante, Gauguin, and DeLorean are exciting to watch. They go "middle-age crazy," wearing new clothes and changing jobs, wives, and philosophies. They rise and fall with pizzazz, startling everyone with their rapid and often ridiculous flip-flops from traditional to avant-garde.

Jess Lair, in his excellent book, *I Ain't Much, Baby, But I'm All I Got,* records his trip through mid-life. A hard-driving businessman, Jess was at his peak making money when a near-fatal heart attack stopped him in his tracks. Realizing that he both needed and wanted to change his occupation, he thought of going back to college and becoming a professor.

What held Jess back is something that holds many of us back: the thought of how old he would be by the time he graduated. "I'll be over 40," he whined. Suddenly the thought came to him, "How old will you be if you don't do it?" This simple thought changed his mind and his life. He went on to graduate, teach, and author several best-selling books.

Less fun to read about are those who respond to the crisis with a whimper. These persons are found in bars or sitting for hours in front of a television. Some are found in mental hospitals, staring at the wall. They are also found keeping stiff upper lips and frozen smiles in homes, jobs, and churches.

Larry was urged to come for psychotherapy by his wife. "I might as well talk to you," he sighed to me. "I've talked to everyone else; besides, I have good insurance." Larry was not a good candidate for psychotherapy. His depression had not responded to drug therapy, had been with him for about 10 years, and had left him without much hope.

Larry went to work everyday, to church every Sunday, and with his wife to obligatory social events. His boss had no complaints; his church thought him a Christian example; his friends just thought he was shy. His wife was the only one who remembered "the old Larry; the one I had fun with. I want him back." She never saw him come back. Larry died sometime after entering therapy, from a cancer that looked very curable. He seemed to just give up living.

Why: "Why Me, God?" "Why Not?"

*T*he Lord in His wisdom made the fly," wrote an anonymous wag, "and then forgot to tell us why." All the religions in the world attempt to answer the great question, "Why is there evil in the world?" Let me attempt to tackle a piece of that question.

There are a few theological "givens" that I will not attempt to debate. If you do not accept these, the rest of the chapter falls short. They are debated elsewhere by countless theologians. (C. S. Lewis would be a good place to start.)

Given No. 1: God created the world without sin or pain (Gen. 1:31).

Given No. 2: Man chose to rebel against God, thus bringing pain and evil upon himself (Gen. 3).

43

Given No. 3: God now uses the inevitable pain and suffering caused by man's sin to mature us and to draw us closer to Himself for our benefit and His own (Rom. 5:1-5; James 1:2-12).

Having condensed three volumes of theology into the above three propositions, let me consider specifically: Why does God use a *mid-life crisis* to benefit His people? The answer is really quite simple: Because it's an excellent learning opportunity. Turn again to Solomon, this time in Proverbs.

> My son, if you accept my words and store up my commands within you, turning your ear to wisdom and applying your heart to understanding, and if you call out for insight and cry aloud for understanding, and if you look for it as for silver and search for it as for hidden treasure, then you will understand the fear of the Lord and find the knowledge of God (Prov. 2:1-5).

How many wise people do you know? I'm not talking *smart;* I mean *wise.* How many people are at peace with themselves, with their world, with their God? With how many lovers of God and their neighbors are you personally familiar? Now, ask yourself one more question: How many of the wise people you know are young? And still one more question: How many of those wise old people sailed through middle age smoothly?

Young adulthood, according to psychologist Erik Erikson, is a time for finding a mate and establishing oneself in an occupation. We busy ourselves with a flurry of activity; raising children is a full-time job in itself. Old age is characterized by the successful or unsuccessful resolution of our life. We either look back with despair on what we *should* have done or with satisfaction on our accomplishments.

So, how do we get from young to old? By passing through the fires of mid-life. My hunch is that those who look with despair on past lives are those who repressed their crises and attempted to live their afternoon with morning values.

The only way to lose illusions is to become *dis*illusioned. The only way to become comfortable with death is to face it. The only way to establish life goals that leave you satisfied in old age is to challenge them. The only way to learn long-suffering is to suffer long. I guarantee the process to be painful. Listen to Job:

> Where can wisdom be found? Where does understanding dwell? Man does not comprehend its worth; it cannot be found in the land of the living. . . . It cannot be bought with the finest gold, nor can its price be weighed in silver. . . . Where then does wisdom come from? Where does understanding dwell? . . . Destruction and Death say, "Only a rumor of it has reached our ears." God understands the way to it and he alone knows where it dwells . . . . And he said to man, "The fear of the Lord—that is wisdom" (Job 28:12-13, 15, 20, 22-23, 28a).

Not that old people are *always* wise. "It is not only the old who are wise, not only the aged who understand what is right" (Job 32:9). Age and a mid-life crisis will not always add up to wisdom; age and a *successful resolution* of the crisis usually will.

"When I was a child," says St. Paul (1 Cor. 13:11), "I talked like a child, I thought like a child, I reasoned like a child. When I became a man, I put childish ways behind me." Judas and Pilate resolved their crises poorly; Paul and Peter went through them and gained the wisdom and knowledge of God.

There's another reason God helps us grow in wisdom: We live not only for ourselves, but for our community and for the kingdom of God. What makes wisdom so individually satisfying is the knowledge that God uses it in the world. He has a purpose for us and, with some wisdom, we can catch a vision of it.

Compare two end products of the mid-life crisis and their sense of purpose: F. Scott Fitzgerald (whom we have mentioned already) and Paul of Tarsus (who probably was in his late 30s when he traveled the road to Damascus). First Fitzgerald:

> This is what I think now: that the natural state of the sentient adult is a qualified unhappiness. . . . I will try to be a correct animal though, and if you throw me a bone with enough meat on it I may even lick your hand. (*The Crackup*, p. 84)

Now St. Paul:

> I have learned to be content whatever the circumstances. I
> know what it is to be in need, and I know what it is to have
> plenty. I have learned the secret of being content in any and
> every situation, whether well fed or hungry, whether living
> in plenty or in want. I can do everything through him who
> gives me strength (Phil. 4:11b-13).

II
Some Easy Solutions (Which Usually Fail)

Whoever has lived long enough to find out what life is, knows how deep a debt of gratitude we owe to Adam, the first great benefactor of our race. He brought death into the world.
—*Mark Twain*, Pudd'nhead Wilson

5

Trying Harder

When in trouble, or in doubt,
Run in circles, scream and shout.
        —Old Navy Saying

So here you are, a mature adult, running your own life. You have a spouse, some children, a career, and some kind of social life. And everything was supposed to be marvelous, happy ever after. But it isn't. And you're miserable.

Nothing makes sense. You're depressed. Life is suddenly very boring. The person sleeping next to you, whom you thought you were crazy about 15 years ago when you met, isn't exciting anymore. Or the family that you thought would fulfill your whole life doesn't. Or the job you thought would be terrific is ho-hum.

You stay up the whole night and cannot fall asleep. Or you fall asleep and cannot wake up. Or both. Or first one, then the other.

Maybe you should see a shrink. Maybe you should take some pills. Maybe you should read the Bible more and pray more. Maybe you should have a baby. You don't know *what* you want.

What you probably will do first is to *chase harder after the great American dream.* "Two cars in every garage, two children, and two jobs in every home—these are the things that used to make me happy. Now they don't, so I'll go for *three* of each.

Nancy and George Novack have been busy since before they can remember. "My mom says that I was *born* moving and haven't stopped since," smiles Nancy. Her high school yearbook lists scores of activities and an A average. When she married George, who was voted most likely to succeed, bets were taken on who would be unable to keep up with whom.

At first, everything seemed to fit. Nancy worked for a time for a well-known architectural firm while George went to law school. Later, when George was well established in a lucrative practice, Nancy had two chidren and continued to free-lance at home. All this while being elected vice-president of the PTA and attending church.

Now, at 40, with the children (Steve and Melody) ready for prep school and George being considered for the state Senate, something is wrong. Their youngest, Melody, stutters and has started having problems at school. George and Nancy are in family therapy with me—more because their pastor recommended me than because they believe in it. They wish I would simply fix their kid, and let them fix their own lives.

GO, GEORGE! GO, NANCY! GO! GO! GO!

Everything in their lives is running smoothly they insist. Money is no problem; they love each other; sex is normal; everything is fine. Speech therapists and child psychiatrists have not dented the problem.

The kids are no help to me either. Both Melody and Steve parrot the party line: everything is fine. They like school, love their parents and each other, and have a lot of friends.

I am getting nowhere fast; and at $50 per hour, the Novaks are understandably upset. But just before they decide to quit, one of those "developmental crises" occurs: Nancy's dad has a stroke.

During the family's next session with me, Nancy is noticeably on edge. She recalls times when growing up that she failed to please her father. "In fact," she says, "I cannot remember *ever* being good enough for him." She begins to cry. "Is this why I spend all my time running, running, running? Hoping that *someday* he will look at me and smile and tell me I did a good job?"

Nancy thoroughly embarrassed her family by breaking down and crying, and they all promptly dropped out of therapy. But, for her, the light had begun to dawn. She realized that she had always competed with George to be busiest. Nancy began to slow down. George tried to understand and accept her changes, but was unwilling to slow down himself. He ran, unsuccessfully, for public office and kept up a vigorous law practice. Nancy, in turn, worked at accepting George's *not* changing, and Melody perked up in school and began successful work with a speech therapist.

> I undertook great projects: I built houses for myself and planted vineyards. . . . I bought male and female slaves. . . .I amassed silver and gold for myself . . . . I became greater by far than anyone in Jerusalem before me. . . . I denied myself nothing my eyes desired. . . . Yet when I surveyed all that my hands had done and what I had toiled to achieve, everything was meaningless, a chasing after the wind; nothing was gained under the sun (Eccl. 2:4-11).

The Shape of Our Economy: Trying for Better

Solomon, as we saw in chapter 2, had it all. And it was not enough. Or, maybe, it was too much. You know, one candy bar tastes great. Sometimes, two taste okay. But, give me three candy bars, and that's too many. I get sick on a good thing. (Maybe you can eat three, but how about 13?) After a while, enough of anything is enough. But, when is that, when translated from candy bars into income?

An economics professor of mine described the "shape" of our economy before the industrial revolution with this illustration:

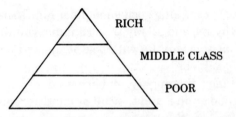

There were a small amount of rich folks, a few more in the middle class, and a substantial amount of poor. In fact, throughout history *most* people have been poor.

Then the professor drew the post industrial revolution pattern of the American economy. The picture has shifted greatly.

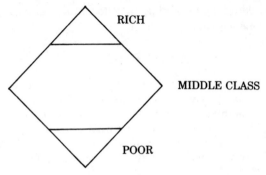

Today, about the same small number of people are rich as before (though "rich" today has a much higher meaning than before); but in comparison to the previous diagram, very few are poor. In fact, only 15 percent of America's people were living below poverty level at the *worst* of the latest economic turndown.

What happened?

The vast majority of the working classes in America migrated from poverty to the middle class. Trade unions, automation, and the minimum wage have all helped to move persons from shacks to suburbs, from dirt floors to wall-to-wall carpeting. Over 90 percent of those original poor have seen their children become comfortable.

The average American now has more money to spend and more time in which to spend it than anyone in the history of the world. We vacation in sunny places, own two or more automobiles, eat out more, and wear better clothing than our ancestors would have dreamed possible. But then the newscasts on our color TVs tell us how bad things are. Has all this affluence made us happy?

It would seem not. We are the most "psychiatrized" nation in the world, buy more drugs (licit and illicit) than anyone else, and have more relatives in mental hospitals than any other nation in the world. Alcoholism damages the lives of one out of three American families, and suicide has become the 10th-largest killer of Americans and the second most frequent cause of death in teenagers.

> Do not store up for yourselves treasures on earth, where moth and rust destroy, and where thieves break in and steal. But store up for yourselves treasures in heaven, where moth and rust do not destroy, and where thieves do not break in and steal. For where your treasure is, there your heart will be also (Matt. 6:19-21).

"There is a burden of care in getting riches," writes Matthew Henry, "fear in keeping them; temptation in using them; guilt in abusing them; sorrow in losing them; and a burden of account at last to be given concerning them" (*Encyclopedia of Religious Quotations,* [Revell, 1976]). I do not think a person can *know* the above truth except by experiencing it. That excludes most children (who usually own very little) and young adults (who often are comparatively poor, still working their way up the economic ladder).

Those of us past 40, however, have seen brand new cars turn into rusted clunkers. We have thrown away tons of old clothing and broken toys. We have witnessed years of fresh bags of groceries turning into smelly bags of trash. Somehow, the thought of buying new stuff loses its excitement.

"Who is rich?" asks Ben Franklin. "He that is content. Who is that? Nobody" (*Poor Richard's Almanac*).

I'm not sure I agree with Ben. I have been poor. Now I am fairly comfortable. I like comfortable better.

My point is not that riches are bad (I enjoy their use), but that riches are not enough. They do not, in themselves, satisfy. To acquire obsessively more when one is already comfortable is a madness, a strangely American madness, typical of the mid-life crisis.

The Shape of Our Bodies: Still Trying Harder

*T*he same persons who madly run around acquiring wealth and social prestige usually will be found also in "the great American body buildup" syndrome. Caught in an endless cycle of dieting and bingeing, overusing and then avoiding the mirror and the scale, starting and quitting tobacco and alcohol, they desperately jog after the sweet bird of youth while it flies away into the sunset years.

We Americans spend millions on cosmetics, plastic surgery, and health spas. We are positively horrified that anyone should see us without makeup or know our weight or age. I love the following dialogue between Norman and Ethel Thayer in *On Golden Pond,* Act I, Scene 1:

> **Ethel:** They're a very nice middle-aged couple. Just like us.
>
> **Norman:** If they're just like us, they're not middle-aged.
>
> **Ethel:** Of course, they are.
>
> **Norman:** Middle age means the middle, Ethel. The middle of life. People don't live to be 150.
>
> **Ethel:** We're at the far edge of middle age, that's all.
>
> **Norman:** We're not, you know. We're not middle-aged. You're old, and I'm ancient.
>
> **Ethel:** Pooh. You're in your seventies and I'm in my sixties.
>
> **Norman:** Just barely on both counts.
>
> **Ethel:** Are we going to spend the afternoon quibbling about it?

Norman: We can if you'd like.

At 39, I attempted to play softball with a church team. I thought I was a passable athlete, but as I practiced with a group of men (boys?) who averaged at least 10 years younger than myself, I came to a stunning conclusion about my body: It was old. They tried to make me catcher. (That's where they play people who can't catch, run, or throw very well in softball.) I demanded to be put in right field. (I couldn't last nine innings with my knees bent, and my arm hurt from throwing the ball back to the pitcher. That's why I asked for right field—the other old man's position.)

Since I was out of shape, I began a regular program of calisthenics and jogging. I did it for two reasons: to get myself in shape, and to lose my potbelly. I began reasonably, at the low end of the plan. I stuck to it, and a year-and-a-half later, I can do 50 push-ups and run two miles. I am now in shape. My belly, however, is as potty as ever, despite the 50 sit-ups I do daily.

Middle-age has crept upon me.

Some Bodily Facts About Aging

As one ages, several things happen that are quite beyond the help of "body builders and aerobics." Eyesight and hearing will be less acute. Speed drops off sharply. Strength, however, will be only 10 percent less at 60 than it was at 25. Hand and finger dexterity decrease. Intelligence stays the same.

This means that older people generally cannot function as well as younger people in jobs that require speed and a quick hand. They learn as well as younger persons, except when the material is presented too swiftly. Their experience, however, is usually great enough to enable them to compete successfully with younger persons on most jobs.

Solomon was not too keen on aging. His comment:

Honor [God] in your youth, before the evil years come— when you'll no longer enjoy living. . . . You will be afraid of heights and of falling—a white-haired withered old man, dragging himself along: without sexual desire, standing at death's door . . . (Eccl. 12:1a, 5 TLB).

An even worse view is taken by Robert Rosenfelt in his article "The Elderly Mystique," *The Journal of Social Issues* (pp.39—41):

Let him [the old man] brace himself for isolation and rejection . . . for loneliness. . . . The nadir of the process is, of course, institutionalization of the aged—not always a necessary or desirable outcome, to be sure, but a practical method of storage until death.

A vicious circle is set in motion. There is no hope in old age, and those who grow old are quite hopeless. That, in essence, is the elderly mystique. Clearly the world pays dearly for this myopic view of what are sardonically called "The Golden Years."

Good news, Solomon and Rosenfelt! It doesn't have to be that bad! Recent evidence shows that there is no natural law demanding our total bodily decline after 45—or 65. Americans are living longer and are staying active longer. Still, as one wag puts it, "Acting as young as you think often leads to feeling as old as you are." When I'm 78, I do not intend to pump iron, as one Helen Zechmeister did, lifting 214.75 pounds from a dead start. I do intend to keep writing, counseling, preaching, gardening, and jogging for the rest of my life. I will do *less* of them when I'm 78, but I will do them till I die because I enjoy myself.

Cecil B. DeMille produced *The Ten Commandments* at the age of 75. Moses was 80 when he wrote them down. And by the way, the Bible reports that Sarah's *pregnancy* was the miracle. Years after she had died and Isaac was married, Abraham married again and sired many other children (Gen. 25:1-6).

There is life after 40. Or 65 even. It is found by those who quit trying so hard. My paunch is permanent. My writing, preaching, and counseling skills are better than ever, but not nearly as good as they're going to get.

How about you?

6

Founding the Clan

Whoso findeth a wife findeth a good thing.
— Solomon (Prov. 18:22a KJV)

A nagging wife is like water going drip-drip-drip.
—Also Solomon (Prov. 19:13b TEV)

It is axiomatic in American culture that marriage and family don't make it anymore. Half of those who marry divorce. Many outspoken writers believe that the vast majority of those who stay together are very unhappy with their marriage. Marriage and family therapy is growing by leaps and bounds. So is the sale of self-help books on the subject.

The grand old man of family therapy, Nathan Ackerman, had this to say about the state of marriage already in 1965:

> It is rickety, its joints creak. It threatens to crack wide open. If marriage is ordained in heaven, it is surely falling apart on earth. Three generations survey the record with dismay. The older married folks look with silent reproach on the younger ones. The younger married folks look at themselves with shocked perplexity and wonder how on earth they ever got this way. The children look at their parents with bitter accusation. "You are wrecking our family. What are you doing to yourselves and to us?" ("The Family Approach to Marital Disorders," *Active Psychotherapy*)

Since the time Ackerman wrote these comments, problems with marriage have gotten so bad (or, at least, so *noticeably* bad) that many marriage counselors are asking each other, "Is marriage over? Is it time for us as a professional group to encourage people who are not married to stay unmarried?"

But 95 percent of the persons in this country *do* marry, at least once in their lives. And four out of five who divorce remarry, most in the first year following their divorce. Obviously, the urge to marry and produce children has not been stifled by the doomsayers. What on earth makes people think that they can beat the odds and live happily ever after?

First of all, there is the romantic illusion of omnipotence held by youth, one of the illusions referred to in chapter 3. Young adults don't believe *they* are going to be like their parents or their friends or like the statistics. Premarital counseling is a joke to most of these starry-eyed dodos. (Pardon my nonprofessional jargon.) They don't come to me (as counselor or pastor) with a problem; they come with a solution, which needs only my perfunctory six sessions (since I require it) and a 10-minute ceremony.

I try. I try to explain the problems, the areas of potential disagreement—money, children, sex, role expectations, etc.—and they just sit there with their youthful smiles plastered on their fresh young faces and let all my wisdom bounce off like a superball. Why? For heaven's sake (literally) and for the sake of their future marriage, *why*? Because they are "in love." They refuse to believe that marriage will be difficult for them.

A second reason people marry is that family provides us with a sense of belonging, a place where, when we go there, they have to take us in. We were born in a family. We fit somewhere in this crazy world; there is a place for us. It might not be the warmest, safest, most pleasant place in the world, but it is *ours*.

We also received an identity from belonging to that family. Maybe we were the black sheep, the good boy or girl, the shy one or the "lover," but we knew who we were—and chances are, we still carry that role today, at least in part. I'm over 40, but the family in which I grew up still calls me "Johnny," and probably always will.

Most people get love and approval (to some degree or other) from their families. Everyone at least gets some attention. I know when I phone my family, they will be interested in why I am calling, what I have done since our last call, and what I plan to do before the next one. Out of several million telephone numbers, there are precious few with persons who are interested in me. Whether I get mad at my family, cry with them, or laugh over someone's latest incident, *I am connected.* I am a Sterner, and that means something. It means that I go to school, read books, attend church, and am interested in the arts. Sterners do that. No one had to tell me to do it; I just *do* it (as do my brothers and sisters, for the most part).

But sometime between adolescence and middle-age, most of us separate from our parents. I joined the navy. I remember it as somewhat exciting, but mostly lonely. I, like millions of other 20-year-olds, attempted to dispel that loneliness by marrying the girl back home. She was living at home and attending college at the time, thinking about *her* separation from her home. My offer sounded attractive.

The person without family will have a tough time finding such a convenient place to get belonging, identity, and attention as in a family. The problem is, that after the two become one, they begin to fight over which one they will be. Carl Whittaker describes newlyweds as "two scapegoats sent out by families to reproduce each other. The battle is over which one it will be" (*From Psyche to System,* p. 368).

A third reason why some people marry is to "found a clan"—a psychologically clandestine way to live forever, at least symbolically. And while they're at it, they'll not repeat the mistakes of their parents. They'll raise perfect kids (or, at least, better than they were/are). The hope of immortality lives on in most parents. But as Whittaker states,

> Every parent fails at bringing up children. No child grows up to be what the parent wants. . . . No matter what they

think they are teaching, the child will grow up to be like the parents [are]. . . . (*Psyche,* p. 375)

Solomon extolled the love of man and woman in his Song of Songs. He liked marriage so much, in fact, that he did it several hundred times. But marriage and family did not seem to satisfy him. "If a man begat an hundred children, and live many years, so that the days of his years be many, and his soul be not filled with good, . . . I say that an untimely birth is better than he" (Eccl. 6:3 KJV). It seems, then, that founding the clan is not enough either.

The young adults having the children don't know that yet. They're too busy tending to their many needs to worry about whether the experience ultimately is fulfilling or not. There are bills to pay, mouths to feed, and bottoms to be diapered. And the babies are so cute. Everyone crowds around them (and the new parents) and oohs and aahs. The babies are important, thus making the parents, too, important—for a short time.

Between 35 and 40, the last of the kids goes to grade school and the first starts adolescence. The kids are no longer cute. They are no longer fawned over by friends and relatives, and they are no longer as dependent on you as before. They begin to experiment with a mind of their own, and they usually begin by questioning everything you taught them. And your chances of immortality through offspring begin to crumble—sometimes with a bang.

"I hate my husband, and I hate my kids," cried Brenda, "and I hate myself for hating them. I hear my pastor preach that the Christian home is the 'Master's Workshop where the character of Christ is lovingly imparted to the children,' and I want to go home and throw up."

Brenda was one of those persons who see their lives as care-givers. Since she was five, she had taken care of people— first her little brother, then the rest of her younger siblings, finally her invalid mother. After her mother died and her brothers and sisters got old enough, Brenda left her father to marry Tom. Fifteen years and four children later, Brenda was on the verge of divorce.

60

"I hate him," she screamed. "He gets to do anything he wants, when he wants, no matter how much it costs or how much it inconveniences me. But it's my own fault," she hastened to explain. "I thought that if I gave him everything, if I did it *right,* he'd appreciate me. Well, he doesn't. And neither do the kids. They're the most selfish, lazy, do-nothing slobs you ever saw."

Brenda represents a lot of us. We thought that after we gave our all to our mates and our children, after we did so many nice things for them, that someday they would thank us, appreciate us. And when they don't, then what?

Throw out the old marriage and start anew? Raise the next family "right" this time with the benefit of your years of marital and parental experience? Many try. They generally report that they have the same problems with the new marriage that they had with the old. Plus new problems with the old family on visiting days and during crises.

My point is, even if you find the end of the rainbow through family, it won't be enough. It wasn't meant to be. Old people know that; young people won't believe it; mid-life is the time for finding that out.

And woe to the children whose parents don't find it out; their parents never let them go. Far into their own marriages, these children are still tied to Mom and Dad. They spend vast amounts of time with them; they go on all their vacations with them; they call them every day, perhaps several times. No important decisions are ever made without consulting the now-grandparents, and large amounts of time and energy are spent wondering whether something will offend them. If *both* sets of parents are afraid to let go, something akin to total insanity pervades the house of their children as they attempt (always unsuccessfully) to please both sets of in-laws.

Somewhere along the line between 35 and 45, we need to come to the conclusion that marriage is good and children can be a lot of fun, but they won't solve all our aloneness problems. Finally, I am the only person on earth who will never leave me. I alone, among all humans, know my secret sins, my desperate hopes, my agonizing letdowns. I may attempt to share these with others, but they will never know or care about them as I do—or as God does.

The amazing thing about giving up the illusion of "eternal life and love" through my family is that now they are *free* to love me. My former demands that they love me were seen as oppressive. My interference in their lives was either resisted or resented. But when I gave up trying to run their lives, they were able to love me, appreciate me, and even ask me for advice.

As another benefit of not living my children's lives, I now have the chance to live my own. Of course, this may be precisely what I have been trying to avoid. Nevertheless, God says that *all* lives are worth living, even mine.

"I thought my mother would die of a broken heart when I informed her that we were no longer coming to dinner three times a week," chuckled Al. "And for a time, it seemed she might. But she got over it. Now, you can't find her at home half the time; she's so busy at church and with her friends. And she and Dad seem to be much happier with each other since we butted out."

How does it happen that accepting my essential aloneness allows me to be more loving and more free? Facing the fact that neither of my families (neither Mom and Dad nor wife and kids) can give me total understanding and love *forces* me to look within to find the kingdom of God at work. I am free to be loved. And my immortality is only in God.

7

Religious and Respectable

A tough but nervous, tenacious but restless race [the Yankees]; materially ambitious, yet prone to introspection, and subject to waves of religious emotion. . . . A race whose typical member is eternally torn between a passion for righteousness and a desire to get on in the world.
> —Samuel Eliot Morison, A Maritime History of Massachusetts

Give me that old time religion; it's good enough for me.
> —Anonymous

Two news articles appeared within weeks of each other in Detroit. I suspect they made the people there who believe in the Bible want either to crawl under a rock or compulsively to grab people on the street and say, "I want you to know that *my* church isn't like that."

The first article, splashed across the front page, reported 11 children severely beaten and 1 child battered to death in a religious camp. The director of the camp said that the children were beaten with the rod of correction, as the Bible directs, in order to discipline them. By court order 66 children were taken from that camp and from their parents who live there.

The second article, also on the front page, headlined, "Was It Murder or Just a Man's Trust in God?" A certain layman was jailed for one year for permitting two of his young children to die unattended by doctors. His pastor, a former respected seminary teacher of theology, was reported as saying, "Doctors will maim and cripple," and "Any of the congregation who go to them should get out of the church! God will give eyesight, healing and even new teeth to those who have faith. Medical treatment of any kind indicates a lack of faith and prevents God from granting healing."

Two things happen to me when I read such stuff. First, I get angry at the obvious foolishness that causes needless death in the name of God. Second, I feel quite proud that *I* am not one of those foolish parishioners, that *I* would never be led into such heresy. I attend a prominent church, I am a mainline Christian pastor and family counselor, I read C. S. Lewis, *Christianity Today,* and Francis Schaeffer. "I thank Thee that I am not as other men are . . . . I fast twice in the week, I give tithes of all that I possess" (Luke 18:11-12 KJV).

It's easy to be self-righteous when there are so many obvious sinners around.

It's also easy to be self-righteous because we want to be right, to be correct, righteous, proper, decent, "with it"—especially in this confusing world. People in general and midlifers in particular often experience disorder in their worlds—including in their world of religion. Conflicting messages about long-cherished values and traditions are frightening.

Some people give up. "What is truth?" asked Pilate as he looked at Truth Incarnate. Most, however, pick a system of theology or philosophy of life (perhaps a cult) and stick to it no matter what the evidence indicates. "My mind is made up," reads the sign, "don't confuse me with the facts."

Using Religion to Find Order

"In the beginning," starts Genesis, ". . . the earth was formless and empty"—"a shapeless, chaotic mass," says the Living Bible. But, "the Spirit of God was hovering over the waters." And in seven days God had created an orderly universe out of that chaotic void.

All religions attempt to bring order into our restless lives. They do this by answering the two fundamental questions of civilization: (1) why is there evil in the world, and why is it not distributed evenly among people; and (2) what happens when somebody dies?

When one wants answers for living and for dying, therefore, one turns to religion. And the God of the Bible has given His people those basic answers for thousands of years. He has *not,* however, given *all* answers to *all* questions. Nor has He always given specific answers for specific cases. Job yelled at God for over 30 chapters. The only answer that this "blameless and upright" man got from God was, "Who are *you* to tell *Me* how to run *My* universe?" (Job 38—41 summarized).

Those who start cults (many of them, like Mary Baker Eddy, in their mid-life) are usually well-meaning men and women who attempt to fill in the cracks that God has purposely left in His Word. They are looking for answers, *all* of the answers, to the hard questions of life. When they cannot find those answers, they invent them.

"The fear of the Lord is the beginning of knowledge," says Solomon (Prov. 1:7 KJV). He further states,

> Wisdom will enter your heart, and knowledge will be pleasant to your soul. Discretion will protect you, and understanding will guard you. . . . Thus you will walk in the ways of good men and keep to the paths of the righteous. For the upright will live in the land, and the blameless will remain in it; but the wicked will be cut off from the land, and the unfaithful will be torn from it (Prov. 2:10-11, 20-22).

It would be easy to conclude that we have here "Solomon's Simple System for Salvation":

1. Fear God.

2. God gives knowledge.

3. This knowledge leads to righteous living, which has two results:

4. God blesses you.

5. And God curses unwise fools who turn to wickedness.

Certainly, there is great truth in Proverbs. But if followed without balance from other parts of Scripture (such as Job, 1 Peter, and James), one gets the feeling that the good guys always win on this earth. Yet, Solomon knew this was not the case—and, in Ecclesiastes, seems overwhelmed by that fact.

> There is an empty thing found on earth: when the just man gets what is due to the unjust, and the unjust what is due to the just. I maintain that this too is emptiness (Eccl. 8:14 NEB).

> In this meaningless life of mine I have seen both of these: a righteous man perishing in his righteousness, and a wicked man living long in his wickedness (Eccl. 7:15).

Solomon's apparent solution to the problem is "do not be over-righteous" and "do not be overwicked" (vv. 16-17). I can understand his admonition not to be overwicked, but why should one steer clear of overrighteousness? Perhaps he anticipated that question out of his own experience: "Neither be overwise—why destroy yourself?" (v. 16).

There Is a Righteousness That Destroys

Jesus said, "Unless your righteousness surpasses that of the Pharisees and the teachers of the law, you will certainly not enter the kingdom of heaven" (Matt. 5:20). Before we "thank God that we are not like they were," we need to understand who the Pharisees were. William Coleman, in his excellent book, *The Pharisees' Guide to Total Holiness,* calls them "the marine corps of Judaism." He writes, "They operated as a highly sophisticated assembly of men who believed they were doing the most important things in all of life" (pp. 6-7).

The Pharisees were so determined not to break the laws of God that they erected a *seyag* (fence) of rules and regulations around that law to help protect it. Imagine their distress when a young rabbi began to break those laws without so much as a second thought, and when asked why, said, "My Father gives Me permission."

Jesus was a threat to their self-made system, as He is a threat to *all* our self-made systems. When we erect fences, He jumps over them with gleeful abandon. And His sayings *are* disturbing. "Sell all you have." "Don't look back." "Many are called, but few are chosen." "If you want to save your life, lose it."

Few people care to think deeply about these and other sayings of Jesus in Scripture. Few people care to think deeply at all. Only during times of pain and problems do most of us wrestle with the serious problems of life. It seems easier to let someone else, some outside authority, do our thinking for us.

The message of the cults (both the Christian, in-group superspiritual groupies and the non-Christian cults) is, "Come unto us, all you who are confused by life's unfairness and disorder, and we will give you a secret, foolproof system to the answers of life and death. Only *we* can give you this knowledge—and we will . . . if you let us have control over your life."

Two groups that head the list of the cultists are often *adolescents* (who are confused as they begin to sort out their values, beliefs, goals, and identities) and *middlescents* (who are resorting those same values all over again). Adolescents are more prone towards non-Christian cults, especially when rebelling against their rearing in Christian homes. Middlescents most often reset their ways in the "old-time religion."

People in mid-life crisis will likely have a profound religious conversion. They may turn from no religion to a strong faith—or vice versa. They may join or get out of a cult, switch denominations, resurrect an old faith, or simmer down from their present one. Or they may switch back and forth a number of times. After all, they are wrestling with issues of life and death—the definition of values, the meaning and purpose of freedom and responsibility and intimacy, and the chilling thought that one is, perhaps, always ultimately alone among humanity. These issues are the warp and woof of religion, and it is natural that one should turn to the church for answers.

What answers are they likely to get?

Answer No. 1: There Is No Answer. This answer is likely to come from a so-called "liberal" church. "I went to my pastor for answers," snorted one of my clients, "and he was having a crisis of his own. He quoted Sartre and Camus and said that I would have to make my own meaning for life; the church had none to give."

Several well-meaning clergymen and some whole denominations have gotten themselves stuck in the hopelessness of Solomon, Job, and the Lamentations of Jeremiah. The fact that those writers did answer a lot of their questions, and that other writers of Scripture answered them also, seems to elude these good people.

When one goes to such a person, she will usually come out more confused and depressed than when she went in. "Make my own meaning?" said my client. "That's what had gotten me into so much trouble in the first place. My meaning of life was not making it; I had no purpose. So I turned to the church—and it has no purpose either." Nonetheless, this client was helped by reading Ecclesiastes and other portions of Scripture and working out a personal relationship with God through Christ.

Answer No. 2: There Is Only Our Answer. Some groups try to address the issue of order and meaning in life by their own version of "Solomon's Simple System of Salvation": "Just come to the altar and pray, and everything will be fine. Have faith. Here is why you are sick and so-and-so is not. Believe! Send me your handkerchief. Pray three hours a day. Give it all to God through me."

Of course, if a person accepts that and then is disillusioned, it's hard to admit it, even to him- or herself. Mike Yaconelli, in his book *Tough Faith,* tells of a group of Christians who were sharing experiences of how God had surprised them. "People were not sharing real experiences," Yaconelli observed. "Instead, they were saying what they thought the pastor and one another wanted to hear" (pp. 3-4).

When Mike shared that "God surprises me by not being around when I need Him, by acting the opposite of what I expect, and by remaining silent when I desperately need Him to say something," the group turned on him. *He had questioned.* "It's not surprising," concludes Mike, "that our churches are filled with sincere, honest people who overflow with sincere, honest questions but never say a word" (p. 5).

Answer No. 3: Work, Work, Work. This answer may be a part of a No. 1 or a No. 2 church. The "liberal" church will get people to collect books for Nigeria, protest nuclear war, teach Sunday school, sing in the choir, etc. The No. 2 church will get its people to witness for Christ, read their Bible x amount per day, teach Sunday school, sing in the choir, etc. There is a vast amount of work to be done in order to keep the church rolling, and the mid-lifer can escape into it just like any other work; except that now he can be self-righteously proud of his "spiritual" accomplishments.

> The easiest place for us to insult God and blaspheme is in the church. The easiest place to lose the meaning of worship is in the worship service, which can become perfunctory and performance-oriented. We may enter and leave a house of worship and never have worshipped at all. (Draper, *Ecclesiastes,* p. 77)

Answer No. 4: All of the Above. In truth, all of the above three answers are correct—and none of them are. The church does *not* have all the answers. No one knows why Jim was miraculously healed and John still limps. No one knows why your baby died or your mother is in such pain or why you got laid off.

This does not mean that the church knows nothing. "We know that we have passed from death to life," writes John (1 John 3:14a). "You know that [Jesus] appeared so that he might take away our sins" (3:5). "We know that when he appears, we shall be like him, for we shall see him as he is" (3:2b). And "we know that we live in him and he in us, because he has given us of his Spirit" (4:13).

There *are* some things that the church knows: God is loving, powerful, and good; because of Jesus' atonement, He loves us; and He works according to His eternal purpose. I am sinful and, therefore, work according to my own purpose. In faith, under the Spirit, God's purpose and mine occasionally match. Sometimes I see the match, and I delight. Often I do not, and I wonder.

8
Getting Smart

*Nothing in education is so astonishing as the amount of
ignorance it accumulates in the form of inert facts.*
    —Henry Brooks Adams,
      The Education of Henry Adams

It was one of those hot summer nights in the year of 1961.
Having recently completed my freshman year in college with
disappointing results, and more recently, having completed a
date with a lovely young thing, also with disappointing results,
I found myself alone in my father's car, parked in an all-night
drive-in theater. It was one of those places frequented by strut-
ting young lads with greasy duck-tailed hair, old jalopies or
motorcycles, and loud music. The "Do Not Get Out of Your
Automobile" sign was being violated joyously.

Though I knew no one in the crowd, suddenly my door
opened and an obviously inebriated youth in a leather jacket
stumbled into my front seat. "Hi, guy," he slurred. "Are you
new around here?" When it was established that I attended
the local community junior college, he was impressed. "Come
on," he slurred as he grabbed me; and I shortly found myself
in the back seat of another father's car. "This is my friend John,"
he announced to his friends. "He goes to college. Go ahead, ask
him anything."

America, that bastion of eternal optimism, has always
placed great hope and expectations in its system of education.
Over 100 years ago, James Lowell remarked (in "New England

Two Centuries Ago," *Literary Essays,* vol. 2), "It was in making education not only common to all, but in some sense compulsory on all, that the destiny of the free republics of America was practically settled." In 1983, a report that declared that American students were *not* progressing but were in fact *regressing* in knowledge shook the nation from president to local public school.

Will and Ariel Durant concluded a lifetime of studying and recording the story of civilization and concluded from it, "Our finest contemporary achievement is our unprecedented expenditure of wealth and toil in the provision of higher education.... We have raised the level and average of knowledge beyond any age in history" (*The Lessons of History*).

The Israelites, too, were big on education. Abraham was probably educated in Ur, as the similarity of the Old Testament law to the Code of Hammurabi suggests. Moses was "educated in all the wisdom of the Egyptians" (Acts 7:22). Jesus could read and was obviously familiar with Scripture. Two of the most highly educated Israelites were Solomon and Saul of Tarsus (Paul). Solomon comments on education:

> Blessed is the man who finds wisdom,
> the man who gains understanding,
> for she is more profitable than silver
> and yields better returns than gold.
>
> She is more precious than rubies;
> nothing you desire can compare with her.
> Long life is in her right hand;
> in her left hand are riches and honor.
>
> Her ways are pleasant ways,
> and all her paths are peace.
> She is a tree of life to those who embrace her;
> those who lay hold of her will be blessed
> (Prov. 3:13-19).

Santa Claus himself could not be expected to give more. Here is promised riches, honor, a long and pleasant life, peace and happiness. One only has to find wisdom. Solomon advises us to seek wisdom like silver and search for it like hidden treasure; and he did what he advised. "I devoted myself to study and to explore by wisdom all that is done under heaven" (Eccl. 1:13a). Solomon was successful in his quest; God granted his desire for great knowledge. "Look, I have grown and increased in wisdom more than anyone who has ruled over Jerusalem before me, I have experienced much of wisdom and knowledge" (1:16).

But what were the results? "I learned that this, too, is a chasing after the wind. For with much wisdom comes much sorrow; the more knowledge, the more grief" (1:17b-18).

Man's Wisdom

*J*ames Draper, in his commentary on Ecclesiastes, believes that Solomon's problem occurred because he was searching for God by using earthly wisdom. "Earthly wisdom only reveals problems—it does not solve them. A comprehensive quest for wisdom soon leads us to understand that we are not achieving anything" (p. 17).

St. Paul makes a similar comment about earthly wisdom. "Has not God made foolish the wisdom of the world?" (1 Cor. 1:20b). "Do not deceive yourselves. If any one of you thinks he is wise by the standards of this age, he should become a 'fool' so that he may become wise. For the wisdom of this world is foolishness in God's sight" (3:18-19a).

As we approach mid-life, it begins to dawn upon us that all of the knowledge we have accumulated is meaningless in the face of death, loneliness, and our loss of illusions. In fact, the hope that education will ultimately result in great human happiness is *one* of those illusions we lose. Paul learned this; he knew that the ultimate solutions to life's problems were to be found through a paradoxical relationship with God through Christ, where one becomes strong through weakness, wise through foolishness, and conquered by submission.

Wisdom and knowledge need to submit to the will of God in order to produce real truth and righteousness. That's problematic enough—but it's even more so when middlescents turn away from the answers of the church (see chapter 7) and turn back toward what they hope will be more satisfying: even more human knowledge. Many mid-lifers, especially women, go back to school. They explore the answers of the sciences, the philosophers, the poets. They look to the old writings of Aristotle, Darwin, and Shakespeare and to the newer ones of existentialism and behavioral biology.

I personally was very upset with the church (as anyone can see by my first book). I began to look to psychology, philosophy, and other writers for answers. I read Rogers, Maslow, Freud, Jung. I went to seminars and weekend encounter marathons. I looked into all forms of psychology, from psychoanalysis to soap opera therapy.

I discovered one thing: they don't have answers either. Listen to some of their comments:

Allen Ginsberg (on the subject of intellectuals): "I saw the best minds of my generation destroyed by madness, starving hysterical naked, dragging themselves through the negro streets at dawn looking for an angry fix." (*Howl*)

Friedrich Nietzsche (on life): "The thought of suicide is a great consolation: by means of it one gets successfully through many a bad night." (*Beyond Good and Evil*)

Jean Paul Sartre (on fellowship): "Man can will nothing unless he has first understood that he must count on no one but himself; that he is alone, abandoned on earth." (*L'Être et le Náeant;* Eng. tran., *Being and Nothingness*) "Hell is—other people." (*Huis Clos*)

Ludwig von Bertalanffy (on changing morals): "We have progressed, in some 5,000 years, from primitive mythology to quantum theory. . . . But it would be a slightly optimistic view that general moral standards have progressed since Lao Tse, the Buddha or Christ." (*New Values in a Changing World*)

Bertrand Russell (on mathematics): "Mathematics may be defined as the subject in which we never know what we are talking about, nor whether what we are saying is true." (*Recent Work on the Principles of Mathematics*)

Sigmund Freud (on psychoanalysis): "Our goal is to turn the hysterical misery into common unhappiness." (*Studies in Hysteria*)

Leo Durocher (on baseball and life): "Nice guys finish last."

I have reluctantly come to the conclusion that the church may not have *all* the answers, but it has more of them—and a better quality of them—than anyone else.

Godly Wisdom

Back to my question: If we keep our knowledge and wisdom pointed in the direction of eternal Biblical truth, can we, then, avoid the problems of Solomon? Was his problem, in fact, that his wisdom was "earthly"?

I think not. "The fear of the Lord is the beginning of knowledge," says Solomon over and over (KJV). We must keep in mind where and how he got that great knowledge [wisdom] in the first place—through answered prayer.

The problem with wisdom runs deeper. There is, I think, something about the getting of wisdom that is inherently painful—which is why most persons who keep themselves "educated" only clog their minds with innumerable facts. "When most people say they are thinking about something," states Dr. Donald Grey Barnhouse, "they are merely rearranging their prejudices" (as quoted by Walter Martin in *Kingdom of the Cults*).

"For with much wisdom comes much sorrow; the more knowledge, the more grief" (Eccl. 1:18). When one sees a thing, *really sees it,* one is bound to leap back in horror and disgust. World War II was a fantasy to me, and remains so, due to the heroic treatment given to it by the newspapers, magazines, and mostly, the movies. It was never glorious to my father, who was there. But, for me, World War II is John Wayne gloriously overcoming overwhelming odds and coming home to marry the girl next door.

Viet Nam was a different business. There is nothing glorious for me about Viet Nam, even though I was never there either. The news media and even the movies portrayed too much truth about that war to make it ever anything but what it was: nasty, horrible, monstrous. From the innocent villagers killed by both sides, to the drug abuse, the political corruption, and the reality of death, Viet Nam was portrayed too truly to be heroic. My new wisdom about death was painful.

When we learn the truth about people, about the history of civilization, or about ourselves, we shudder. Is it any wonder that most people have no idea of what's going on and no intention of learning? "As scarce as truth is," writes Henry Shaw (in *Affurisms*), "the supply has always been in excess of the demand." Who among the young want to understand, become wise about pain, suffering, or death?

Lucy had come to me with an intense fear of driving, which began shortly after an almost fatal accident on the highway. It is not unusual to be a bit anxious after such an incident, but Lucy could not bear to get into an automobile. This fear was too acute to be a simple case of stimulus-response. The fear turned out (after some months of therapy) to be related to the death of her father some years earlier and the anger and rejection of her mother when Lucy got married. To Lucy, both of her parents had died, one physically and the other socially. The auto accident was simply the "trigger event" that activated Lucy's death anxiety.

"But I've never even thought about dying," said Lucy doubtfully when I gave her this interpretation. "And besides, what's my mother not speaking to me got to do with death?" Lucy, like all of us, was well defended against thoughts of death. Yet, when she faced her own mortality, her fear of driving vanished. The wisdom and knowledge was painful, like a surgeon's knife. The festering had to come out. Then the healing could take place.

One of my favorite Bible heroes (he's also mentioned in Hebrews 11) is Jacob. If he can be a great man of faith, so can I. Jacob was so named ("Tripper," or "Supplanter,") after he was observed catching onto his brother Esau's heel in childbirth. Jacob lived up to his name as he supplanted Esau by buying his birthright for a pot of lentils and by tricking his father, Isaac, into blessing him instead of his brother. When Esau became enraged, Jacob lit out for his uncle Laban's country.

Laban was a cheat, too; and Jacob found himself serving him for 14 years and getting two wives, instead of 7 years for Rachel as he had intended. By that time, the two cheats found that Laban's part of the country wasn't big enough for both of them, and Jacob started back for home. As he approached familiar territory, word came back to him that Esau was coming to meet him—with 400 men. Jacob panicked. Behind was Laban, to whom Jacob had promised never to return. In front was an army. In times like that, people pray.

Jacob wrestled with God all night and told Him, "I will not let you go unless you bless me. The man [God] asked him, 'What is your name?' 'Jacob,' he answered. Then the man said, 'Your name will no longer be Jacob, but Israel, . . .' " (Gen. 32:26b-28). God asks, "What is your name? Who are you, *really*?" Jacob must answer, "I am Jacob—a cheat; I cheated my brother and my uncle, and now I'm scared." And the changing of his name implied, "You admit who you are; now you can be changed."

"Repent!" demands Jesus. "Look into yourself and admit the garbage that is there. Admit that it is there because you *chose* it; *you,* not your parents and not your spouse, decided to be what you are. Repent, for the kingdom of God is at hand!"

Lloyd Alexander writes "children's literature" that I love to read. One of my favorite stories, *The Foundling,* tells of a young man named Dallben. Three black-robed hags find him in the Marshes of Morva. One wants to eat him, but the other two prevail—and so baby Dallben grows into a young lad.

When it comes time for Dallben to leave and seek his fortune, the hags offer him a present. He selects from their various treasures a book containing all knowledge and wisdom. He takes the book gleefully and begins to read of things he had never dreamed about.

> But he had finished less than half when the pages, to his horror, began to grow dark and stained with blood and tears. For now the book told him of other ways of the world; of

77

cruelty, suffering and death. He read of greed, hatred, and war. . . . Each page he read pierced his heart.

Dallben thinks to destroy the remainder of the book, or at least refrain from reading it, but something pushes him to continue. The book goes on to tell of birth as well as death, how one day ends so that another can begin, and that each person's life is a priceless treasure, and in the end,

> while nothing was certain, all was possible. . . . "At the end of knowledge, wisdom begins," Dallben murmured, "and at the end of wisdom there is no grief, but hope."

"The truth shall make you free," reads a bumper sticker, "but first it shall make you miserable."

You may attempt to escape the mid-life crisis through obsessively cramming endless facts into your head. I doubt that it will work. If it is *wisdom* you seek, however, the result will be an intensification of the mid-life crisis—which will also lead to a successful conclusion. But only after much pain.

"The fear of the Lord is the beginning of wisdom" (Ps. 111:10a).

9
Turning On

Ay, in the very temple of delight
Veil'd Melancholy has her sov'ran shrine.
　　　—John Keats, "To Autumn"

Is this it? Are we having fun now?
　　　—Carol Burnett, in the film The Four Seasons

"If I have any more fun, I think I'll throw up!" Betty chuckled, but she looked tired around the eyes. It's hard to lie with your eyes, but she wasn't really trying anymore. "I can't stand the pace," she said quickly. "Find a sitter for the kids; run home from work; get dressed; get to the party; go to bed with my lover; then get up and try to sneak home without waking up the kids. Next day, it's back to work with four hours sleep. I sometimes long for those long, endless nights in front of the TV."

Betty was a casualty of her husband's mid-life crisis. Morris was a basic, middle-class good guy for 15 years of marriage. "He took out the garbage, gave me his paycheck, and made love to me every Saturday afternoon," stated Betty. "Once in a while he took in a ball game or went somewhere with the church men's group. Never had more than two drinks from the day I met him. We visited his parents or mine every Sunday.

"Then, all of a sudden, he snapped. He went crazy. Started staying out late, smelling like perfume and beer when he came home. He drank more around the house and started buying marijuana—from his own son! Finally, he said he couldn't stand it anymore, that he'd found somebody else. He quit his job—I don't even know what state he lives in now. He told me he'd worked all his life for his parents, for me, for the kids. Now he was going to get something for Morris."

At first, Betty responded to her husband's changes by denial. "He'll snap out of it," she had thought. "It's just some kind of phase." Then she got angry, suspicious, and demanding. By the time I saw her, she had gone through several "phases" herself. "I figured, what the heck. If he can have fun, so can I." But the fun was starting to wear out.

Alternating Between Martyrdom and "Me First"

"If it feels good, do it" was the byword of the 70s. Those in midlife had some real problems with the "me" generation. They had been raised to believe that Christians put other people first. Various Bible verses were quoted to support this. Then along came this huge bunch of baby-boomers looking, not for commitment, but for fulfillment. Divorce rates soared; drug use became passé, thousands of true believers flocked to pseudo-psychotherapists who advised them to "lose your minds and come to your senses."

Morris and Betty were just two of the casualties of the "me" movement. Books are now being written and university courses taught on the subject of what to do for the *children* of "me-oriented parents"—parents who divorce when the marriage doesn't turn them on anymore, who are spaced out on drugs or alcohol, or who constantly desert their children for social events.

Songs and movies are made about people like Betty, the "middle-age crazy" husband or wife who leaves it all for "true" love, self-actualization, or a condo in Hawaii. It makes great copy, not so great lives. Psychoanalyst Leon Saul calls these "the dangerous years," when marriages are broken up without thinking, only to wish years later that "we'd had a little more sense."

The problem with running away from the straight life of paying your taxes, taking the kids to scouts, and watching TV with the family on Saturday night (according to James Dobson) is that a person tends to return to it again as soon as the dust settles. And the new flame soon becomes the same old, fire-breathing dragon.

In fact, an amazing number of those who divorce remarry somone just like the spouse they rejected. At any Al-Anon meeting you'll find women who married two or more alcoholic men (or vice versa). Psychoanalysts call this the "repetition compulsion," the need to repeat one's past. This may account for the fact that almost 70 percent of those who remarry divorce again.

The middlescent who divorces and remarries may be looking for the same things she was looking for as an adolescent—which encourages the repetition compulsion and another divorce. People who keep looking for that "perfect match" or the "one love that will make everything right" are doomed.

Solomon was in the unique position of not needing a divorce in order to have variety. He simply added to his huge stable of wives and concubines whenever the mood struck him.

> I acquired men and women singers, and a harem as well— the delights of the heart of man. . . . I denied myself nothing my eyes desired; I refused my heart no pleasure (Eccl. 2:8b, 10a).

Solomon spared no expense to bring himself the best and most exotic of all the pleasures the world could offer. He was, after all, Israel's greatest importer and businessman, and he resolved to share in all of the delights that were available.

> I thought in my heart, "Come now, I will test you with pleasure to find out what is good." But that also proved to be meaningless. "Laughter," I said, "is foolish. And what does pleasure accomplish? " . . . Yet when I surveyed all that my hands had done and what I had toiled to achieve, everything was meaningless, a chasing after the wind; nothing was gained under the sun (2:1-2, 11).

Sigmund Freud has proposed that all of human life is based on the "pleasure principle," that is, the instinctive seeking after pleasure and avoiding pain. In earliest life, he reasoned, people tend to fulfill their desire for pleasure immediately. Maturity means that people gradually learn to postpone pleasure until a later time. In other words, quick pleasure is just that: quick.

When asked what were the marks of a mentally healthy human being, Freud said, "The ability to work and to love." The pleasure that seems to last in life is that which we get from working meaningfully and from relationships that are loving. Those middlescents who look back on years of little fulfillment in either of these vital areas are likely candidates for the mad chase after quick, cheap thrills.

Many mid-lifers attempt to escape the crises of meaning, aloneness, and death by a flurry of activity. These persons are similar in nature to those workaholics referred to earlier, except that they lose themselves in fun—parties, snowmobiles, vacations, and of course, television.

The average American watches from three to four hours of TV per day. There are families who sit nightly before the sacred box, speaking only to discuss what to watch next (and then in hushed tones), their eyes set straight ahead on the latest "star."

These people are ill-equipped to handle the real world. They are being taught by TV that any crisis can be solved in under one hour. They see millions of commercials for things they don't need and cannot afford, but which they "must" buy to be happy. These people view hundreds of thousands of violent deaths, rapes, and bloody fights. In short, instead of living life, they watch a caricature of it.

And what of those who don't watch that much TV?

In half a century Americans have gone from working 12 to 14 hours a day, six days a week, to a 40-hour week. We have more vacation time, sick time, and paid holidays than any other people at any other time in history. And now we are seriously considering the four-day work week. What will we do with our time—we, the "leisure society" (the current name for a large group of people who have, or soon will have, more time to play than to work)?

What sort of meaningful response will we give to that opportunity?

Horse racing, ice skating, jogging, Kabuki dancing, leather work, mountain climbing, needlepoint, ornithology, quoit, racquetball, overeating, philately, quiz shows, rowing, sun bathing, tennis, undersea exploring, volleyball, weight lifting, X-rated movies, yard sales, z-z-z-z-z-z.

A Story: Once upon a time, there was a man and his wife who were poor and who had to work all the time. "O God," they used to pray, "if we had more money and more spare time, we could give it to You and to Your work." And God heard their prayer, and He gave them more money and more spare time. And they went to Florida and bought a new air-conditioned automobile with FM stereo and push-button windows. They watched their favorite movies on cable TV and took up sailing. And God saw, and He took the money and the time away. And the couple prayed, "O God, if we only had time and money, we could do great things for You here on earth." And God said, "You gotta be kidding!"

During the recession of the early 80s, with more Americans out of work than at any time since the 1930s, we *still* found several millions of dollars to shove into hungry video games. Our dogs and cats ate better than almost one-quarter of the world's human population.

By any reasonable historical standard, we are incredibly endowed with time and money. What has America to show for it? And how have we invested our God-given talents? Mostly, we've hidden them under a tree.

According to a recent article in *Esquire,* young people in this country are bored and lazy. They are afraid of commitment to anything and afraid of not being committed to anything. They are afraid of being sucked into an endless pursuit of money (which might leave them with insufficient leisure time) and afraid of not having enough money to enjoy their leisure time.

How much money is enough? Just a little bit more.

— J. Paul Getty

Some of us, however, cannot take all this free time and easy money. It sticks us somewhere in our mid-western, Protestant work ethic. (I'm told by reliable sources that California Catholics and New York Jews have the same guilt pangs.) But help is on the way, friends! The pseudo-psychotherapists of the world have banded together to get rid of all our guilt.

They do this by absolving us from the sin of feeling responsible for anyone but ourselves. "Win through intimidation!" "Look out for number one!" "The sky's the limit!" "Learn how selfishness can be a virtue!" "Read the latest book offered to relieve you of all your silly guilt."

Gail Sheehy writes of a man who had been to such therapists and read this type of literature. She quotes,

> Yes, I'm devoted to number one. That's correct. I have nothing to lose at this [mid-life] stage except maybe money. So, I don't give a _____ what I do as long as it pleases me or gives me strokes. (*Pathfinders*, p.44)

This man, according to Sheehy, was "a dagwood sandwich of every processed shortcut to self-love that California's human potential packages have concocted" (*Pathfinders*, p. 44)

A Better Path to Enjoyment

T hat still, small voice of guilt ought *not* be "therapized" away. We are guilty because we have been sinful. "What did you do with the one talent I gave you?" asks our Master. "Well, . . ." we say, "I had a real good time."

> Depart from me, you who are cursed, into the eternal fire prepared for the devil and his angels. For I was hungry and you gave me nothing to eat, I was thirsty and you gave me

nothing to drink, I was a stranger and you did not invite me in, I needed clothes and you did not clothe me, I was sick and in prison and you did not look after me (Matt.25:41b-43).

Let me state loud and long that God is pro-pleasure. "Rejoice in the Lord and be glad, you righteous; sing, all you who are upright in heart," says David (Ps. 32:11). "Enjoy life with your wife, whom you love," adds Solomon (Eccl. 9:9). Even Jesus must have enjoyed life; He was named a glutton and a drunkard by some (Matt. 11:19). In fact, our problem may be that we aren't having *enough* fun (of the right kind) to please God.

"I am come that they might have life, and that they might have it more abundantly," says Jesus (John 10:10 KJV)—more true fun, more true pleasure, more meaning and purposeful living. I am distressed when I see churches full of people who seem to be having less fun that those persons in sports arenas, shopping centers, or bars. Where is our "abundant life"?

I find one of the key answers to this in Hebrews 11:25, where the writer brags that Moses, by faith, "chose to be mistreated along with the people of God rather than to enjoy the pleasures of sin for a short time." *For a short time.* That's the problem with less-than-Godly pleasure.

When we spend our money, we look for, as one important ingredient, how long a thing will last. We rustproof and wax a new automobile. We choose clothing that will wear longer. And we want our entertainment to last, too. "It was a neat ride," said my daughter of an amusement park offering, "but I liked the one better at X park; it lasted twice as long." (But I know that even the latter was measured in seconds.)

All pleasure is short-lived, except for the joy we get in doing the will of God. It seems to warm us over and over again as we reflect on it in our memories. I never shall forget my first congregation of elderly, mentally handicapped, and blind and deaf persons in a Sacramento nursing home. Those dear saints appreciated me more than has any other group before or since. I turn those moments over and over in my mind and smile.

There are other moments that I turn over with sadness, remorse, or disgust. They were pleasurable at the time, but somehow, they don't taste very good today. I wish they'd go away. Perhaps in heaven I will be able to forget them as God has.

Most of my so-called pleasurable moments, however, *are* forgotten, simply because they were so *unimportant* in the long run of my life. As I approach old age, I pray for the wisdom to fill the remainder of my life with moments worth remembering—now and in heaven.

Having written these noble words, I still want to catch the rest of the Lion's game. "The good that I would . . . ."

10
Dropping Out

Don't think—drink!
—Sarcastic Saying of AA

What do we do after trying respectability, religion, hard work, family, education, and more fun than is fun? What do we do when nothing works, when we still feel empty and meaningless, that our whole life has been vanity and striving after the wind? Many quit trying.

Dropping Out with Drugs and Demon Rum

"I tried cheering myself with wine," says Solomon (Eccl. 2:3). Actually, most mid-lifers drink *less* alcohol and take *fewer* non-prescription drugs than younger persons. But for those who have solved problems in the past by dropping out chemically, the problem solidifies in middle age. And although young people are praised for "holding their booze" or "sowing their wild oats," older people are pitied or scorned.

Solomon had a conflicting attitude toward the use of alcohol. On the one hand, he warns in Proverbs against its abuse.

Who has woe? Who has sorrow?
Who has strife? Who has complaints?
Who has needless bruises? Who has bloodshot eyes?

Those who linger over wine,
    who go to sample bowls of mixed wine.
Do not gaze at wine when it is red
    when it sparkles in the cup,
    when it goes down smoothly!

In the end it bites like a snake
    and poisons like a viper.
Your eyes will see strange sights
    and your mind imagine confusing things.
You will be like one sleeping on the high seas,
    lying on top of the rigging.

"They hit me," you will say, "but I'm not hurt!
    They beat me, but I don't feel it!
When will I wake up so I can find another drink?"

(Prov. 23:29-35)

This sounds as if Solomon had firsthand knowledge about giving himself to wine. His brilliant ridicule of those who overindulge has been read at countless AA meetings all over the world.

However, another passage by Solomon disturbs those of us who counsel about the human wreckage of alcohol.

Let them drink and forget their poverty
    and remember their misery no more (Prov. 31:7).

Many commentaries concentrate on the verse preceding the one just quoted, in which those who are dying and in pain are to be given alcohol to dull the senses (as Jesus was offered on the cross). They completely ignore verse 7, in which Solomon offers alcohol to the depressed, bitter, or afflicted in soul for the purpose of forgetting their problems.

The problem with this advice is *not* that it doesn't work; it works *too well*. For tens of centuries, alcohol has been known to be an excellent method of temporarily dulling pain—both physical and emotional pain. But the cure soon turns out to be worse than the disease.

A person starts his or her affair with alcohol (or any other type of harmful drug) as a search for pleasure. After a time the person begins to rely on the alcohol or drug for relief of unpleasant thoughts and feelings. After a longer time the person must drink just to feel normal. The drug is now master.

> And if I drink oblivion of a day,
>> so shorten I the stature of my soul.
>>> —George Meredith, "Modern Love"

Doug Swanson had a problem. In fact, several problems. "My wife left and took the kids," he said as he began the list. "She says she has no respect for me anymore. I guess I should find a job, but I get unemployment, and I can hustle a few nontaxable bucks to make up the difference. I guess we just don't communicate anymore. I don't seem to care about anything, and I've gotten real moody."

His wife, Jean, however, gave me a markedly different impression of Doug's problems when I called her. "He's drunk every night," she rasped angrily. "He screams at me and the kids constantly, makes sexual jokes in front of my friends, and passes out every night in front of the TV set. I didn't realize how bad he was until he was laid off. Now I've seen him as he really is, and I'm getting out."

Doug had grown up in a family that drank to socialize and to solve problems. He listed several of the relatives on his family chart as "drinks too much sometimes." He admitted to himself and to me that he "occasionally drank a little too much," but denied that he was an alcoholic. Just to please me, however, he attempted several times to cut out drinking altogether. He failed.

After he was arrested for drunk driving and his license was suspended, Doug began to think that Jean might be right. He voluntarily completed an alcoholism rehabilitation program at a local hospital.

Upon graduation, he resumed his therapy with me and began attending AA meetings two or three times a week. Only then did he begin to face the problems of loneliness, guilt, resentment, and his ultimate demise—those mid-life issues that plague all who are sober long enough to think about them. "You know, Doc; sometimes I think I should go back to the bottle. That always turned off these weird thoughts."

Dropping Out of My Mind

Some mid-lifers (thankfully, a small minority) are driven crazy by the force of their inner and outer stresses. One now elderly gentleman stepped out of his house one day and, instead of walking to the bus stop as was his custom, walked into his own world. It is a fascinating world, with its own rules, customs, and even its own language. After 30 years he has never returned from that world, despite all of the psychiatric drugs, behavior modification, and psychotherapy the various hospitals could give him.

One of my clients spent two weeks each year in the mental hospital throughout her mid-life. "Vacations I can't afford; the funny farm my insurance will pay for." Actually, her case was more serious than she jokingly let on. But, I wondered, what would have happened if she'd ever learned to face and fight her issues instead of bottling them up and then blowing up once a year.

Arnold Mandell, a psychiatrist, writes about the coming of *his* middle age:

> For the first several years of my professional life I knew what I was doing. . . . As I approached thirty-five, the fervor started to burn out and I began not to understand. . . [Sometimes psychotherapy worked and sometimes it didn't.] Things became dada. . . . Something has happened to the psychotherapy that I used to think was a good idea. Or has the something happened to me? (*The Coming of Middle Age*)

Dr. Mandell temporarily went insane as a reaction to the stress of a heart attack. Before coming out of it, he escaped from his room and became the venerable Dr. Sam Shambhala, specialist in the mid-life crisis, driving the hospital out of its institutional mind. (After all he was a doctor there.)

Dropping Out with Depression

Most mid-lifers don't react as strongly as Dr. Mandell. He went into the crisis with a shout; most whimper through it with depression, the "common cold" of mental illness. Most everybody gets it at some time or another. At mid-life it seems as though it could be fatal.

Mark (from chapter 1) had problems getting to sleep at night. He would toss and turn and finally wake up the next morning feeling exhausted. He alternated between periods of gluttony and no appetite at all. At work and at home he had no energy, no desire to do anything. "Nothing's fun anymore," he complained, "not even sex." Mark felt hopeless, unworthy, sad, and guilty. "I can't say what I'm sad or guilty *about,* Doc, but I feel that way most of the time."

Sometimes the depression is serious enough that psychiatrists prescribe medication, such as tricyclic antidepressants. (These are not to be confused with tranquilizers, like Valium, and are not addictive. Nevertheless, they should never be taken except under the direction of a competent psychiatrist.)

Sometimes the depression gets so bad that hospitalization or electro-convulsive ("shock") therapy is required.

And sometimes the malady *can* be fatal. Each year, thousands of mid-lifers commit suicide. Most were depressed for a long time. Some sought help from friends and family. Most were told to "snap out of it." They snapped.

Dropping Out with Religion

A local pastor meant well when he wrote a tract entitled, *You Can Win Over Depression.* Part of it reads:

> Don't allow depression to linger for any great amount of time. Adjust your life, your situation, your thinking and your vocabulary quickly. Place yourself in the hands of God as quickly as you can. The moment you know you are in the hands of the Lord, . . . the depression will flee on the wings of the morning.

Another thin booklet (by a different author), *Ten Steps to Victory Over Depression,* advises, "Always be positive." "Seek first the kingdom of God." And "In everything give thanks."

I can just hear the typically depressed mid-lifer reading those two booklets. "Heaven knows, I've *tried* to be positive and thankful and to seek God's kingdom. I would just love to 'adjust my life' so as not to allow depression to linger. I have adjusted my situation—several times—but the feelings still won't go away. How can I now place myself into the hands of the Lord? There must be something *horribly* wrong with me, or the depression would have 'fled on wings' by now."

By contrast, Norman Wright's helpful booklet *An Answer to Depression* points out that Moses, David, Elijah, and Jonah were all afflicted by depression (Num. 11:10-16; Ex. 18:12-22; Ps. 51; 77; 1 Kings 19:1-18; Jonah 4:1). These are hardly faithless, ungodly, hardcore, unrepentant sinners! Listen again to Solomon:

> So I hated life, because the work that is done under the sun was grievous to me. All of it is meaningless, a chasing after the wind. I hated all the things I had toiled for under the sun . . . . So my heart began to despair over all my toilsome labor under the sun. . . . What does a man get for all the toil and anxious striving with which he labors under the sun? All his days his work is pain and grief; even at night his mind does not rest (Eccl.2:17-18a, 20, 22- 23a).

We really don't understand how evil we and others are till mid-life. As infants, we are blissfully unaware of evil. As teens, we overemphasize to the point that, as young adults, we drop the whole matter of evil. The issue then smoulders and burns until mid-life events ignite the mess into a thunderous discharge that will not be ignored. Then, with David and Paul, we know that,

> There is no one righteous, not even one;
> there is no one who understands,
> no one who seeks God.
> All have turned away,
> they have together become worthless;
> there is no one who does good, not even one.
>
> Their throats are open graves;

their tongues practice deceit.
The poison of vipers is on their lips.
Their mouths are full of cursing and bitterness.

Their feet are swift to shed blood;
ruin and misery mark their ways,
and the way of peace they do not know.
There is no fear of God before their eyes.

—Paul quoting from the Psalms (Rom. 3:10-18)

We Can Overcome, But . . .

*W*hat, then, do we do with the very real and depressing issues of loneliness, responsibility for our life, our search for meaning amidst the chaos of the world, and our ultimate death? We can go either on the "wide path" with Saul, Cain, Judas, and the rich young ruler or on the "narrow path" with Jacob, David, Paul, and Thomas.

Life *is* depressing. It *is* enough to make a person drink or go crazy. "In this world you will have trouble," promises Jesus (and I know of no one who argues with this part of the verse). "But take heart! I have overcome the world" (John 16:33). We can either concentrate on the tribulation and stay depressed, or we can concentrate on Jesus' overcoming and, with His Spirit, work through it.

Warning No. 1: This overcoming will be costly. It cost our Lord His life—and He warns us to expect the same.

Dietrich Bonhoeffer coined the phrase "cheap grace" to sum up the popular religion of our times.

Cheap grace is the preaching of forgiveness without requiring repentance, baptism without church discipline, Communion without confession, absolution without personal confession. Cheap grace is grace without discipleship, grace without the cross, grace without Jesus Christ, living and incarnate. (*The Cost of Discipleship,* p. 47)

People in general and Americans in particular are used to having everything served up to them instantly and in disposable containers. Our comforts, our relationships, and our attempts to answer deep life-shattering questions are disposable and instant. But wisdom, like grace, is costly.

Bonhoeffer continues:

> Costly grace is the treasure hidden in the field; for the sake of it a man will gladly go and sell all that he has. It is the pearl of great price to buy [for] which the merchant will sell all his goods. It is . . . the call of Jesus Christ at which the disciple leaves his nets and follows him. (p. 47)

> It's not my father,
> not my mother,
> but it's me, oh, Lord,
> standin' in the need of prayer.
>
> —American Spiritual

Warning No. 2: Overcoming will not come quickly. "I die daily," says Paul. Those who overcome go through the fire of purification again and again.

One of my dear old friends, a saint in her 70s, used to say upon hearing my various problems, "God's just killing you out, John, like He does me, because He loves us." After hearing this for over 10 years, I remarked that she must be almost dead by now. She burst in retort, "I haven't *begun* to die yet!"

The overcoming comes slowly. It was ever thus. For some, it takes so long that it seems hopeless. (But it isn't.)

> "This is why I told you that no one can come to me unless the Father has enabled him."
> From this time many of his disciples turned back and no longer followed him.
> "You do not want to leave, too, do you?" Jesus asked the Twelve.
> Simon Peter answered him, "Lord, to whom shall we go? You have the words of eternal life" (John 6:65b-68).

III
The Difficult Solutions (Which Usually Work)

Everything that happens in this world happens at the
*   time God chooses.*
He sets the time for birth and the time for death, the time
*   for planting and the time for pulling up,*
the time for killing and the time for healing, the time for
*   tearing down and the time for building.*
He sets the time for sorrow and the time for joy, the time
*   for mourning and the time for dancing,*
the time for making love and the time for not making
*   love, the time for kissing and the time for not kissing.*
He sets the time for finding and the time for losing, the
*   time for saving and the time for throwing away,*
the time for tearing and the time for mending, the time
*   for silence and the time for talk.*
He sets the time for love and the time for hate, the time
*   for war and the time for peace.*
*   —Solomon (Eccl. 3:1-8 TEV)*

11
Relating to a "New" God

"Then he isn't safe?" said Lucy. "Safe?" said Mr. Beaver. "Don't you hear what Mrs. Beaver tells you? Who said anything about safe? 'Course he isn't safe. But he's good. He's the King, I tell You."
> —C. S. *Lewis,* The Lion, the Witch and the Wardrobe

The young preacher smiled, closed his Bible, and stepped toward the congregation. "Are there any questions?" he asked. For two weeks, night after thrilling night, he had kept the faithful spellbound with his series on the "soon-coming Christ." His meticulous charts on Ezekiel, Daniel, and Revelation had by now spread clear around the front of the church. He had told his willing listeners exactly how, if not exactly when, Jesus Christ would return for His church. There were no questions.

After a closing hymn, an older preacher made his way to the front of the sanctuary. He waited patiently as the young man shook the hands of the well-wishers and collected his notes and charts. At last he eased over to the young man's side. "There is one question in my mind," the older man said slowly.

"Sure," beamed the younger preacher. "What would you like to know?"

"Well," said the older, "if our Lord were to choose to return to this earth in some other manner than you have outlined, you wouldn't be angry with Him, would you?"

The young man was stunned. He was without words for the first time in two weeks. Most men are when they consider God in a way that doesn't fit perfectly with their preconceived notions. "My ears had heard of you," says Job, "but now my eyes have seen you. Therefore I despise myself and repent in dust and ashes" (Job 42:5-6).

There were Bible scholars in Jesus' day, too. No doubt they read, discussed, reread, and discussed some more the passages which they believed applied to the coming Messiah. They had figured out just how the Messiah would come, what He would do, and how He would establish the Kingdom of David forever. They were wrong.

Is Our God Too Small?

J. B. Phillips, in his wonderful book *Your God Is Too Small*, writes:

> No one is ever really at ease in facing what we call "life" and "death" without a religious faith. The trouble with many people today is that they have not found a God big enough for modern needs. . . . It is obviously impossible for an adult to worship the conception of God that exists in the mind of a child of Sunday school age, unless he is prepared to deny his own experience of life. (p. 7)

Phillips goes on to list the "small gods" of modern times. Some of them are the "Grand Old Man," who sits and smiles while His children do as they please; the "Resident Policeman," who looks about angrily for someone having too much fun; the "Parental Hangover," from our youth; and the "God-in-a-Box," whose ways are perfectly explained by whichever group is doing the explaining. All of these and other small gods, Phillips asserts, are inadequate to the task. He urges us to "fling open the windows of our minds" and let in the light of Christ.

Don't try to understand me—just love me.

—T-shirt on a local boy

Jeffrey had been in therapy with me for what seemed like a very long time for both of us. He was, according to the *Diagnostic and Statistic Manual of Mental Disorders,* 3d ed., a classic "301.82—Avoidant Personality Disorder." In other words, he wished to relate to others, to love and be loved by them, but he was afraid of rejection.

He had spent his last several holidays sitting in front of a television set, while his relatives wondered why he ignored their dinner invitations. He had never had a girlfriend. His job consisted of counting stock in a warehouse; something he could do all day by himself.

Jeffrey was extremely religious. He never missed church, though he would come in late (well after the congregation shook hands with one another) and leave during the closing hymn. His concept of God was "the Big Man," a phrase he also used to describe his father.

I had tried all my psychological tricks on Jeffrey, and the therapy was going nowhere. I was discouraged; he took it with gallows humor ("I never expected much in the first place"). Nevertheless, he was stuck with me. I was his only friend, even though a paid one—of which he never ceased to remind me.

He was an obedient client. He came on time and paid punctually. He read everything I told him to read. One day he came into my office, after reading some book or other, with a smile on his face and a spring in his step. I was a bit shaken and asked what had gotten into him.

"I just discovered that God loves me."

"Oh . . . yeah?" I responded brilliantly.

"The book, the one you gave me—it says that God loves everybody; right?"

"Uh-h-h, right."

"Well, *I'm* part of everybody. So—God loves me!"

The euphoria only lasted a few days. Jeff still had to confront a lot of issues in his life. Dating was extremely fright-

ening. Just going out to restaurants and places of entertainment was difficult. But he was no longer alone, sepa-
rated from "the Big Man." God loved Jeffrey, and relations with
God's world were now possible. Jeff is still kind of a nut; but
he's a more lovable nut—and a lot happier one. He found a
bigger God.

In the book *Mister God, This Is Anna,* a six-year-old ex-
plains that we go to church to understand God *less* (i.e., to find
a "bigger" God).

> You go to church to make Mister God really, really big. When
> you make Mister God really, really, *really* big, then you
> really, *really* don't understand Mister God . . . . When you're
> little, you understand Mister God. . . . You can ask Him for
> things; He can strike your enemies deader than a doornail;
> . . . Mister God is so understandable, so useful, and so usa-
> ble. . . . In whatever way or state you understand Mister God,
> so you diminish His size. He becomes an understandable
> entity among other understandable entities.

God Is Big Enough to Find Us

Grow in the grace and knowledge of our Lord and Savior
Jesus Christ," urges Peter (2 Peter 3:18). What will this growth
look like? How will the God that is too small seem to those who
let Him get bigger? I suggest the following ways:

1. He will be more mysterious.
2. He will be less easy to manipulate.
3. His laws for living will be harder to enumerate clearly.
4. His ways will be more demanding than you ever imag-
ined.
5. He will be found to love you more than you ever dreamed
possible.

The book *Understanding God* is, I'm told, very helpful as
a catechism. Nonetheless, its title prevents me from reading
it. The title reminds me of the little Sunday-schooler drawing
a picture of God. When reminded that no one knows what God
looks like, she remarked confidently, "They will when *I* get
done!"

As one primary difference between Himself and the gods of other Semitic tribes, Jahwe specifically demanded that He not be idolized. "You shall not make for yourself an idol in the form of anything in heaven above . . ." (Ex. 20:4). Why not? Why is the simple carving of wood or stone to represent God so repugnant to Him?

Psalm 115 gives some insight into the reason. "Our God is in heaven; he does whatever pleases him. But their idols are silver and gold, made by the hands of men. . . . *Those who make them will be like them*" (vv. 3-4, 8a, italics mine).

Have you noticed that pictures of Jesus tend to reflect the race and culture of the painter? We have a blond, blue-eyed Jesus, a black Jesus, an Indian Jesus. We have a very famous picture of the Last Supper, painted with Jesus and His disciples sitting about an Italian table, which was unknown to the Jews of that time.

When people make representations of God, they consciously or unconsciously make Him to be like them. Thus, a Republican makes a conservative God; a guilty person imagines a wrathful, vengeful God; and a lawbreaker believes in a nice old man who looks the other way. Some of the ultrafeminists refer to God as "she."

Who Is God, Anyway?

I used to have a friend who, if you quoted certain parts of Scripture to him, would say, "That's a Baptist verse." (My friend was not a Baptist.) That, for him, would end the argument. As the various denominations, preachers, and especially the cults have amply demonstrated, you can make any kind of God you want, if you read only the parts of Scripture you like.

Scripture, however, places the God of mercy right beside the God of justice; the God of the Law sits by the God of grace. Paul insists, "A man is justified by faith apart from observing the law" (Rom. 3:28). James replies, "Faith by itself, if it is not accompanied by action, is dead" (2:17).

Solomon says that we'll *never* understand God completely. "He [God] has made everything beautiful in its time. He has also set eternity in the hearts of men; yet they cannot fathom what God has done from beginning to end" (Eccl. 3:11).

"God is best known in *not* knowing Him," writes St. Augustine (*De Ordine,* II 16). "We can know what God is *not,* but we cannot know what God *is*" (*De Trinitate,* italics mine). God makes the same point about Himself:

> "My thoughts are not your thoughts, neither are your ways my ways," declares the Lord. "As the heavens are higher than the earth, so are my ways higher than your ways and my thoughts than your thoughts" (Is. 55:8-9).

Truly, when we let Mister God get as big as our minds can take, He is found to be doing "wonders that cannot be fathomed, miracles that cannot be numbered" (Job 9:10). However, this *inscrutability* of our God (as it is termed in theology) does not get us off the hook. "The secret things belong to the Lord our God, but the things revealed belong to us and to our children forever, that we may follow all the words of this law" (Deut. 29:29). All of God and His will for us that He wants us to know can be known, if we are willing to search for it.

> I got the "gimmie-God" blues.
>   I got the "gimme-God" blues
> 'Cause God won't give me what I choose.
>   I got the "gimmie-God" blues.
>
> —Anonymous

"Did you know," Linus asks Charlie Brown, "that if you hold your hands upside down, you get the opposite of what you pray for?" Of course, this is ridiculous—isn't it? After all, we know that the Lord does whatsoever He pleases (Ps. 115:3; 135:6). Yet, if one looks at a large, loud minority of preachers, one is led to believe that if the correct incantation can be found and uttered with enough faith, God will be forced to do as the *"incantor"* pleases.

It is as if God were the Great Computer in the sky, and we humans were the "hackers." Our job is to find the secret password that will open up the Great Computer's program so that we can play the game and get what we want.

Solomon knew better. "I know that everything God does will endure forever; nothing can be added to it and nothing taken from it" (Eccl. 3:14). The fact that Solomon knew this may have been one of his problems. In spite of all his riches, power, fame, and wisdom, he could not get God to do anything that God chose not to do.

"What is Your name?" asks Moses of Jahwe in the burning bush. "I am who I am," answers the Lord (Ex. 3:14a). It was popularly believed that if you knew someone's name, you had a certain amount of power over that person. God, then, is saying, "You don't get power over Me; I have power over you. You don't have to know My name; I already know yours."

Writing to psychologist William James, Justice Oliver Wendell Holmes Jr. stated, "The great act of faith is when man decides that he is not God" ("Letter to William James," 1907).

And What Does God Want?

*I*n some ways, the will of God for His people is very simple. Love the Lord your God and your neighbor as yourself. Do unto others as you would have them do unto you. Stop doing evil and learn how to do good. Read Scripture; pray; attend church; tend to the widows and orphans; show mercy and justice.

Several Scriptural "laundry lists" of sins and righteous actions (especially in Paul's letters) expand on the will of God for daily living. Perhaps the most popular is Galatians 5:19-23.

The problem for God's people is not "what to do and what not to do" in a *general way*. It is rather how to apply the fruits of the Spirit in *specific* ways and situations. Some examples from my office:

A certain woman's husband sexually molests their children and physically beats her. He must be removed from the family, but the woman has no way to earn a living on her own. The county welfare office says she must file for divorce before they can give her any aid. Her pastor and family maintain that divorce is out of the question no matter what.

A teenager feels that he is called to be a missionary. His parents are against the idea; but then they usually have been against their children's ideas. They have bitterly opposed any of their offspring leaving home for whatever reasons and did not attend either of their older children's weddings. The young man is caught between wanting to obey his parents and what he believes to be the will of God.

A couple can't agree on whether to have Grandma live with them or go to a nursing home. Grandma wants to stay in her own home. The county social worker says he will put Grandma in a home if the couple does nothing.

I could spend all day listing such examples—and so could you. I know of no easy, cookbook approach (which works) to these kinds of problems. "The problem with daily ethics," Dr. J. Harold Ellens told me, "is that we are usually not given an easy choice between good and evil, but rather a choice that will be partly good and partly evil no matter *what* we do."

As Mister God gets bigger, we learn that His choices for us are hard choices and that often He seems to stand by and let us make the wrong ones.

There is one right choice to make; but again it's general: it is to answer yes when Jesus says, "Follow Me." But with our limited, human understanding, following Jesus can sometimes be like looking at Him through foggy glass. Yet, we follow Him, even though it will certainly lead to tribulations, persecution, and perhaps death.

A rich young man once told Jesus that he had kept *all* the commandments since he was a child. Our Lord didn't dispute him; that would have led to an endless argument. Jesus merely asked that he give all of his money to the poor. Then He watched the young man walk slowly away (Matt. 19:16-22).

As I get into middle age, I realize that I have not kept all of Jesus' requirements, or even any completely. I remember that little old lady (mentioned earlier) in a prayer meeting singing, "I surrender some," because she wanted to be honest with God. At times, my honest song would be, "I don't surrender a thing tonight, and I haven't for a long time; but keep hanging in there, God, and I just might."

He Wants to Love Us

One of my usually depressed mid-lifers recently floated into my office with a Cheshire cat grin on her face. "No problems today," she chuckled. (She is married to an alcoholic who has been seeing other women.) "I feel just great!"

"Why?"

"I just heard a preacher on TV say, 'You know what? God loves ya, and He's not even mad at ya.' "

The good mood she has will last only for a time, but if the *message* holds, she is beginning to understand life in the kingdom of God.

I think it takes till mid-life to understand how much God loves us. Jesus told a story about a man who was owed 500 denarii (1 denarius equals 1 day's wage) by one debtor and 50 by another. He decided to cancel both their debts. "Now which of them will love him more?" Jesus asks Peter.

"I suppose the one who had the bigger debt canceled," he replied.

"You have judged correctly," Jesus said. Then he turned to "a woman who had lived a sinful life in that town," who had brought on the story by pouring precious ointment on his feet. Jesus said, "Her many sins have been forgiven—for she loved much. But he who has been forgiven little loves little" (Luke 7:41-47).

I have been forgiven much. Some sin is public and obvious to all. Some has the good fortune of being covered up by friends and family. Some is known only to me—and to God, and He loves me anyway. And He's not even mad at me.

Solomon's greatest problem seems to be that he forgot about God's forgiveness and love. (I argue here on the shaky ground of his silence.) I suggest that Solomon knew quite well about the great sinfulness of man: "There is not a righteous man on earth who does what is right and never sins" (Eccl. 7:20). There is, however, no mention of the mercy of God in

Solomon's writings. The word *forgiveness* is never used; and Solomon refers to God's love only to illustrate His discipline.

Perhaps Solomon never felt the need for God's forgiveness. Perhaps it never occurred to him. After all, he was blessed by God with fabulous riches, wisdom, fame, and power. (I realize I'm out on a theological limb, but . . . perhaps.) If so, his spiritual descendant could be the church at Laodicea (neither hot nor cold) to whom God spoke through John, "You say, 'I am rich; I have acquired wealth and do not need a thing.' But you do not realize that you are wretched, pitiful, poor, blind and naked" (Rev. 3:17).

God's love is not blind. He sees right through my feeble defenses, excuses, and shams. He reads my heart, even the pornography and violence that I take such great pains to conceal from everyone, including from myself. (Especially myself!) Yet, He loves me, the real me. The mid-lifer needs to know this more than at any other previous time.

This "new" God that begins to be seen in mid-life is hard to get along with. He keeps demanding things I never thought of before. He shows me sins in places where I never even knew there were places. It's as if I have to be born again, all over. He isn't at all dependable in the ways that I want Him to be.

"Trust God?" smiles my little old lady friend. "You can't trust God. As soon as you think you have Him all figured out, BAP!—and He's got you, boy."

Trust my childhood view of God? No. Trust the inscrutable God, who loves me because of Jesus, in spite of who and what I am? Yes!

With Peter, where else can I go? He loves me. He knows me, and He still loves me. And He has the path—He is the Path—to eternal life.

12
Relating to a New "Me"

It's hard to be hip over thirty when everyone else is nineteen.

—*Judith Viorst,* It's Hard to Be Hip Over Thirty,
and Other Tragedies of Married Life

When my wife says to me, "You're not the man I married, John Sterner," boy! is she right. I was 20 years old, weighed 165 pounds, and wore a crew cut. I was in the navy, lived in Maine (when the navy let me), and attended the Presbyterian church. I intended to graduate from college one day and *be* somebody.

Now I am Dr. Sterner, the psychologist, author, and sometimes preacher. My hair is longer and grayer. I have returned to the Presbyterian church after 20 years in four different denominations. I am in my mid-40s, and what I weigh is none of your business.

I am also getting older. (Considering the alternative, it's not such a bad deal.) I like my generation. It may be a tad slower, a lot grayer (or balder), and more wrinkled, but we own a lot of the world and run most all of it. Ninety percent of the U.S. Congress is over 40. People in their 40s earn about twice what people make in their 20s. We over-40s also drink less alcohol and commit less crime than young folks.

I also think I'm getting better in a number of ways. I am having more fun with life than I ever have before. I love more people and love them more deeply. I am wiser, more patient, and more willing to see where I am wrong than I was at 20 (or even at 30). I am less likely verbally to blitz someone for being wrong (i.e., for disagreeing with my position). I can tell someone no and make it stick, without feeling guilty. I am more at peace with God, with my soul, and with my fellows. (By the way, I'm also more humble than ever before.)

The above sounds as though a committee should be gotten together to canonize me or bronze me or something. But you can check with my family and close friends; I'm still *very* human. I'm not perfect, but I am better. But then, when I was 20, I had a lot of ways to *get* better.

What Makes a "Me" I Can Relate To?

Gail Sheehy, after writing *Passages,* was determined to find out what the differences were between those persons who successfully negotiated the crises of life and those who were crushed by life's events. She handed out a yes/no questionnaire to over 60,000 persons that contained statements such as:

1. My life has meaning and direction.

2. I have experienced one or more important transitions in my adult years, and I have handled these transitions in an unusual, personal, or creative way.

3. I rarely feel cheated or disappointed by life.

Ms. Sheehy published her results in the book *Pathfinders.* She found that those who scored most highly overall on this test of well-being were

more educated than average;

married;

satisfied with their job;

from every economic class; and

more likely to speak of having a faith.

Let's analyze those five points in terms of a new "me."

In chapter 8 we looked at education as a way to survive mid-life crisis—and found it wanting. Nevertheless, as Solomon says, "Get wisdom, get understanding . . . . She will set a garland of grace on your head and present you with a crown of splendor" (Prov. 4:5a, 9).

You may not ever get a doctor's degree, but you can be *educated*. My wife, with no degrees, reads constantly. Every week she totes piles of books home from the library. Since she has chosen to educate herself in a different area from mine, our daily walks have become times of sharing, debate, and mutual learning.

Marriage, the second Sheehy finding, was covered in chapter 6. Again, while it's not enough, it sure contributes to my well-being. The relationship of God and His Son to the human race is consistently compared in Scripture to the marriage bond. Here on earth there is no other relationship which affords anywhere near the opportunity for love, repentance, and growth. "Marriage," says a local mother of 10 children, "is the only chance for the average person to exhibit heroism." It is also capable of producing a lot of fun.

Sheehy's list includes a satisfying job. I suppose that history will record that the greatest tragedy of the industrial age was that it dehumanized work. But it doesn't have to. You simply have to find (if possible) the work you enjoy.

"Why do you do what you do?" an interested person asked me recently. "Is it the money, the prestige, or what?"

"I love it," I answered. "I cannot wait to get to work." To those of you who are able, I urge you to consider *first* the meaningfulness of your future employment, and second the salary. Ms. Sheehy and many others have found that economic factors are much less important than how the employment fits the person.

Most importantly, Ms. Sheehy found that "in every group I surveyed, people of high well-being were more likely than the others to speak of having a faith." She is supported here by Alcoholics Anonymous, countless studies reported in professional journals, and by such eminent psychologists as Victor

Frankl, Irwin Yalom, and Carl Gustav Jung, the latter of whom stated that *all* of his adult patients had at their core a religious problem.

Ralph sat slumped in the chair across from me, wringing his hands in the gesture of helplessness that I had come to know quite well. "What-am-I-gonna-do-Doc?" he said over and over. "I'm working my head off to make everyone happy, and no one's happy."

"Why don't you work a bit to make *yourself* happy?" I suggested.

"I can't," he insisted. "There's so much I *have* to do that I never get the chance to do what I want to do."

Ralph would have flunked Ms. Sheehy's test miserably. In fact, he did everything miserably. Later, I thought, what's the difference between Ralph and me? We are about the same age and make about the same amount of money. He says he likes his work; both of us are married with four children; and both of us are people who spend most of our waking hours working on some project or other. I'm happy and he's miserable. How come?

I subsequently came up with a number of differences; but one of the most important was that Ralph had no faith. There was no one who loved him all of the time, no one who would never leave him nor forsake him, no one to give ultimate purpose to his life. Without faith in God, one must face up to total aloneness in the world. Without God, all love is conditional; if you do this or act that way, then you will be approved and loved. If not, forget it. Without God, life is empty and death is terrifying.

The Importance of an Adult Faith in Christ

The kind of faith Gail Sheehy found in successful mid-lifers was an individual, personal faith in God. It was less prescribed by the church or inherited from childhood. It was more thought out. It often had recovered from bouts with agnosticism or a falling away. In other words their faith had been stimulated by periods of doubt.

Ralph's wife was driven by her church in much the same way that he was driven by his work. Nothing was ever quite good enough for Norma's God. No matter what she did or how hard she tried, Norma always felt that God disapproved. In the same way that Ralph never got his jobs done "right," so Norma never got her religion "right." Ralph had not grown up in a religious home and was not impressed by Norma or her church. Norma's concept of God had not grown up.

"It is for your good that I am going away," says Jesus. "Unless I go away, the Counselor will not come to you . . . . You will grieve, but your grief will turn to joy" (John 16:7, 20b). If Norma had only been willing to lose her earlier concept of God, she might have developed one that would have been more joyful to herself and more appealing to Ralph. St. Paul experienced that. "When I was a child, I talked like a child, I thought like a child, I reasoned like a child. When I became a man, I put childish ways behind me" (1 Cor. 13:11).

Successful mid-lifers have let go their childhood image of Jesus—in order that a deeper image might replace it. They are willing to "see through a glass darkly" with their faith so that someday they will see God face to face. They are able to put up with "knowing in part," and they wait to "know even as I am known."

Ralph, with no faith of his own and the poor example of Norma, had decided to devote himself to his family. All had gone well till his mom and dad died. When he turned his full attention to Norma, she didn't want that much of it. So, he miserably devoted himself to jobs that he thought would please her—but which never did. His life had no meaning, no real direction beyond the next job, and no fun.

Dr. Mandell (still in the delusion that he was the great Dr. Sam Shambhala) goes to see a 70-year-old colleague about midlife crisis. Dr. Hammer tells Mandell that life is less stressful, more enjoyable, and a lot more fun at 70 than it was at Mandell's age. The solution is in giving up.

"How can you call it giving up when you got so much more productive?"

"Ah, that's the point. It's the easy doing of giving up. It flows. After your fear goes away, there isn't any more work. Just activity."

That's the difference between Ralph and me. He is driven to work; I have fun with it. And it started with surrender. Just whom Dr. Hammer surrendered to, I have no idea. But I know whom I surrender to. And each time I do, I feel the power of it. "When I am weak, then I am strong."

The Power of God for Change

Dr. Irvin Yalom tells of a terminal cancer patient who finds that his impending death has helped him to "trivialize the trivial—and pay attention to the truly important things in my life."

If my mid-life shake-up did anything for me, it was that. Some things that I once thought were important now have slid into the background. Others, like looking at a sunset with my wife or reading a good book, have gotten more important. My values have changed.

Not only that, my *ways* of valuing have changed, too. I no longer decide what's "good" or "bad" on the basis of what other people think, or what they will think of me if I decide this way or that. I care less for "law and order" kinds of value judgments and more for ethical values that are consistent with Scripture's view of God in Christ. I recently read an old Bible of mine and wondered at the passages that I had underlined some 10 years ago. Today, I would highlight different passages.

My reasons for liking people have changed also. I can now like those who are not so nice to me. For instance, I have a real affection for a lady in an institution who has never said a kind word to me. I can enjoy those who are different from me, even those who cannot enjoy me because I will not be what they want me to be. I can even admit the possibility that some of my adversaries may be right and that I may be wrong about some things. (But they'll still have to convince me.)

I believe that my changes are profound and are a direct result of experiencing God in the middle of my mid-life re-evaluation. Men like Isaiah, Ezekiel, Moses, and Simon Peter were never quite the same after the experience of meeting God. Abraham left his home; Jonah went to Nineveh; Peter became a rock; and Job shut up. Those who successfully survive mid-life with faith in Jesus understand life better from God's perspective. And things look different from there. Now I can trivialize the trivial and get on with my work in the kingdom of God.

Now for the bad news. (I had to give you the good news first, or you might never have finished the chapter.) In order to experience this better relationship with the new me, I had to accurately assess the old me. In order to "put on the new self, created to be like God in true righteousness and holiness," I had to recognize that there was an "old self, which is being corrupted by its deceitful desires" (Eph. 4:22b, 24)—an old me that needed changing.

God cut through my denial of this old self by using my mid-life crisis. As I wrestled with the reality that I and I alone was responsible for my life, that I was responsible for the vanity and the striving after the wind, then God began to show Himself—and myself—to me. I began to lose my illusions about what a nice guy I was. I began to see that *my* heart was corrupted by its deceitful desires.

I have heard theologians disagree whether a person must first acknowledge the nature of God or first the nature of man. Whichever; both must be present in order for repentance to occur. (I am not writing here about that first step of salvation, but about the subsequent life of sanctification and living abundantly in the kingdom of God.)

"The law was given through Moses; grace and truth came through Jesus Christ" (John 1:17). It has been my experience that, in order to receive more grace, I had to receive simultaneously more truth—truth about who God is, truth about who I am. The crisis of mid-life was no fun for me, but it certainly gave me great opportunities to repent.

Norma and Ralph, to my knowledge, still are under law. Norma is under church law; Ralph is under those unwritten rules handed down by his parents and grandparents. Neither will admit the truth about themselves, for neither understands God's law nor really believes in grace. Thousands and thousands of Ralphs and Normas exist in this world. I wish I had some surefire psychological techniques or prayers to change them.

Solomon had a hand on God's law.

> There is not a righteous man on earth who does what is right and never sins. . . . God made man upright, but men have gone in search of many schemes. . . . God will bring every deed into judgment, including every hidden thing, whether it is good or evil (Eccl. 7:20, 29; 12:14).

What a stinging reminder of the need for repentance!

If that were not enough, a second burr has lodged itself under my psychic saddle for most of my mid-life. It is still there. It's called "confusion." I am terribly afraid of confusion. I want to know what is what. I like black and white; yet I find myself in a world of shifting grays.

As I began to question my values, my logical premises, and my theological and psychological positions, confusion reigned. Was I right or wrong? Did I need to repent? If so, from what? And *to* what? Was I partly right and partly wrong? If so, which parts were which?

Before I could repent "successfully" (that is, in psychological-theological jargon, to come up with an altered state that was pleasing to God and which fit my newly developing self), I had to deal with the confusion. The problem was, the only Bible passage that immediately came to mind said, "God is not a God of confusion" (1 Cor. 14:33 RSV).

I considered, therefore, that my confusion was a sure sign of spiritual weakness or that God had deserted me. And I remained confused, despite my prayers that God take it away. Thank heaven I finally remembered that the verse is talking about how to run a worship service, not about mental or emotional confusion. I felt a great burden lifted.

114

There is some evidence that any new learning is preceded by what Alfred North Whitehead calls an "imaginative muddled response"—confusion. When an idea or response does not fit neatly into our collection of ideas, we must sort out those ideas, readjust some, and throw away others. This process is painful, for we must admit that we were wrong. It is also a lot of work. It is much less painful and laborious simply to discard the new idea.

During a TV show Bill Cosby related his experience with first-grade math. The teacher says, "One and one is two." "Great!" thinks Cosby, "what's a two?" If intellectual ideas are difficult to integrate into the system, emotionally charged ideas are murder. And any idea that challenges my ideas about God, my righteousness, mom, baseball, or apple pie is bound to be defended against. (Don't worry, though. If God cannot get you to listen to His still, small voice, He has a bigger one.)

When the dust settled and I began to be more at home with my imaginative, muddled responses, I understood God. That is, I understood that He is not understandable. Nevertheless, I found Him to be closer, bigger, yet somehow warmer and friendlier than before. He *likes* me!

Knowing that God *likes* me, *loves* me because of Jesus, I can be at peace with the God who confuses me, who cannot be totally understood, who seems so distant when I search, yet delights to sneak up on me when I least expect Him.

> Go, eat your food with gladness, and drink your wine with a joyful heart, for it is now that God favors what you do. . . . Whatever your hand finds to do, do it with all your might, for in the grave, where you are going, there is neither working nor planning nor knowledge nor wisdom. . . . A man can do nothing better than to eat and drink and find satisfaction in his work. *This too, I see, is from the hand of God* (Eccl. 9:7, 10; 2:24, italics mine).

I wonder if Solomon, with all his riches, power, and wisdom, felt the certainty of life after death that any humble follower of Christ knows.

> Just as we have borne the likeness of the earthly man, so
> shall we bear the likeness of the man from heaven. . . . We
> will not all sleep, but we will all be changed—in a flash, in
> the twinkling of an eye, at the last trumpet. For the trumpet
> will sound, the dead will be raised imperishable, and we will
> be changed. . . . Thanks be to God! He gives us the victory
> through our Lord Jesus Christ (1 Cor. 15:49, 51-53, 57).

But consider: Since we do have the clear assurance of God's
love and forgiveness because of Christ—and the assurance of
life with him after death—how much are we responsible to live
with Him in God's kingdom *now* and receive the abundant life?
"From everyone who has been given much, much will be demanded" (Luke 12:48).

> The older I grow, and I now stand on the brink of eternity—
> the more comes back to me that sentence in the Catechism
> I learned when a child, and the fuller and deeper its meaning
> becomes: "What is the chief end of man? To glorify God and
> enjoy Him forever." (Thomas Carlyle)

13

Relating to a New (?) World

Today change is so swift and relentless in the techno-societies that yesterday's truths suddenly become today's fictions.

—*Alvin Toffler*

Mark (the one I mentioned in chapter 1) said, "Solomon said that there's nothing new under the sun. *There* is where I disagree with him. Maybe there was nothing new under *his* sun, but there sure is under mine. My mom sold the family homestead and moved to a senior citizens' complex in Arizona, where she's now a political activist in the Gray Panthers.

"My son wears an earring, and my daughter is thinking about joining the army," he went on. "My church supports revolutionary groups in Africa; my lodge admits women; and my barber is now a hair stylist. My job description didn't even *exist* 10 years ago and probably won't exist 20 years from now. In order to be successful in world business today, you need to speak English, Japanese, and computer. Nothing new? Everything's new!"

From one perspective, Mark is correct. For most of unrecorded history, people lived in caves or huts and hunted, fished, and gathered the abundant wild vegetation from their land. As the game and vegetation played out in one area, the groups simply packed up their few belongings and moved to another. (There are yet a few food-gathering societies left; notably the !Kung San of the Kalahari Desert in southern Africa.)

The food gathering society gave way to the agricultural society because the wandering tribes kept wandering into each other's way. And a brand-new situation was invented by the human race: private property. With the advent of owned property, governments became more necessary, powerful, and complex—and wars more frequent. The agricultural mode of living held forth until about A.D. 1850-1900.

Although inventions, such as writing, gunpowder, and the printing press, partly changed the way of living; much remained the same. You could usually count on living in the same community with your childhood friends, believing in the same things you always did, and working in the same job as your parents. Life was not idyllic, but at least it was predictable. Says Tevya proudly in *Fiddler on the Roof,* "Because of our traditions, everyone knows who he is and what God expects him to do." But even Tevya's world collapses when his third daughter, Chava, announces her engagement to Fyedka, a Gentile. Tevya forbids. Chava elopes. Later, when Chava begs her father to accept her marriage, he cries out to heaven, "Accept them? If I try to bend *that* far, I will break. On the other hand . . . there *is* no other hand. No, Chava. No-o-o!"

Tevya walks slowly away while Chava pleads, "Papa; Papa!" The chorus sings slowly, "Tradition; tradition; tradition." Tevya never speaks to his daughter again.

As early as 1800, the industrial revolution began changing the lives of great masses of European and American people. Jobs began to be outside the home. Farming, which had occupied over 95 percent of these families before 1850, was the job of less than 5 percent of them by 1950. Children now had little or no idea of what their fathers did for a living, but they were taught (consciously or unconsciously) that it was much more important and exciting than what their mothers did.

The new jobs created more income and more leisure time for the family. This, together with great strides in the quality of health care, which caused longer average lives, resulted in thousands of free hours for the average person. Many of these hours, especially for the young, were beginning to be spent in the pursuit of education. Soon, most everyone could read.

The Price of the New: Dealing with Change

On the surface, the above looks like extremely good news. It is referred to as "The Great American Dream." It is not, however, without a price. Leo Tolstoy, going through his great depressions, which were brought about by his reflections upon the lack of meaning in the world, observed, "The peasants do not seem to experience this problem" (paraphrased from *My Confession, My Religion, the Gospel in Brief*). Only when the masses have Solomon's idle time can they experience his "vanity and vexation of spirit" (to use the KJV terms from Eccl. 1:14).

Along about 1900 came mass transportation and mass communication. The family began to disperse, especially in America. (All but one of my five brothers and sisters and all but one of my aunts and uncles are located in states different from the one in which they were born.)

Religious, governmental, and familial authority also began to dwindle. People looked to writers of books and to famous personalities for direction. Madison Avenue replaced Pennsylvania Avenue as a source of values. Anything old—including old people—was suddenly no good; "disposable" and "instant" were the qualities sought after in products and relationships.

Kingdoms, too, changed. Many of the names on the maps that I studied as a schoolboy do not exist today. Some countries have changed their boundries as well as their names.

Society changes its fads, fashions, rules, etiquette, and ethics in a flash. By the time I have learned the latest teenagers' jargon, they have dropped it. Not even the Joneses can keep up with the Joneses.

·

Women's place in the scheme of things drastically flip-flopped. From the right to vote, through the discovery of "the pill," to the National Organization of Women, *both* men and women have had to adapt to radical changes. Now there are house-husbands, and a woman has run as a candidate for the Vice-Presidency of the United States.

In 1970, Alvin Toffler told us in his book *Future Shock* that the changes were happening at a greatly accelerated rate. His own book, according to him, was already out of date *by the time it was printed*. He predicted that this accelerating rate of change would cause breakdowns in communication among average people, a misreading of reality, and an inability to cope.

Toffler was partly right, if the huge amount of media space devoted to "stress" and "burnout" is any indication. But only one decade later, Toffler himself was saying that the industrial revolution was itself being replaced rapidly by the "third wave" industries of "microchips and services."

John Naisbitt, in his book *Megatrends,* reinforces Toffler. Naisbett lists 10 *new* directions that he believes will significantly change our lives. The moves are as follows:

1. From a heavy industrial-based to an information-oriented society. In 1950, only 17 percent of all workers held information- oriented jobs. By 1982, the number had risen to 60 percent.

2. From a "forced technology," mass production, unionized work force to a "high tech/high touch," individualized, more personal, computerized, and smaller industrial work force.

3. From national economic policies to a world economic view.

4. From short-term profit making toward a long-term ecological view.

5. From centralized to decentralized decision making in government and business.

6. From dependence upon institutional help with problems toward self-help.

7. From a representative democracy toward a participatory democracy.

8. From hierarchial, authoritarian structure toward "networking" structures in which each employee or citizen participates in the decision-making process.

9. From living in the Northeast toward living in the Southwest and in Florida.

10. From simple either/or solutions toward multiple options and individualized solutions.

It is the 10th trend (from either/or to multiple options) that has created many of the problems that I hear about in my office everyday. People have too many choices. They don't know what to do with all this responsibility. They are panic-stricken lest they make the wrong choice; guilt ridden when they do.

What is the *Christian* position toward homosexuals? How about the position of women in the ministry? What about nuclear disarmament? Television? Alcohol? Video games? Is there a clear-cut, Biblical position on any or all of the above? What of abortion, welfare, divorce, bussing to achieve racial balance? How about ecology, mass advertising, leisure time, hunger in the Third World nations? How does our present hostility toward Japanese imports square with the ethic of "turning the other check"?

There *is* a Christian ethic toward society—toward the above questions and others—but it isn't as clear-cut for every question as we would like.

Life and times change. Solomon was well aware that his kingdom was temporary.

> I hated all the things I had toiled for under the sun, because I must leave them to the one who comes after me. And who knows whether he will be a wise man or a fool? Yet he will have control over all the work into which I have poured my effort and skill under the sun. This too is meaningless (Eccl. 2:18-19).

As it turned out, Solomon was right to be pessimistic. His son Rehoboam divided the kingdom and lost forever Israel's status as a world power.

God's kingdom, however, "is an everlasting kingdom, and [his] dominion endures through all generations" (Ps. 145:13).

"Repent," cries Jesus, "for the kingdom of heaven is near" (Matt. 4:17). John counsels, "Do not love the world or anything that belongs to the world." Why? Because "the world and everything in it that people desire is passing away" (1 John 2:15a, 17a TEV).

Are Values Permanent or Temporary?

"Value turnover," claims Toffler, "is now faster than ever before in history. While in the past, a man growing up in a society could expect that its public value systems would remain largely unchanged in his lifetime, no such assumption is warranted today." Value turnover? "God says that His righteousness is *everlasting* and His law is true (Ps. 119:142).

Will and Ariel Durant remind us that some societies of ancient history were very moral; others were not. Some values, such as the desired number of children and the divine rights of governments, have changed a lot. Others, such as the right to private property and the sanctity of human life, have not.

As C. S. Lewis states in *The Abolition of Man,* there are some universal values which have not changed since at least the discovery of writing. These include:

1. Kindness towards one's fellows.
2. Special kindness and duty to one's family and country.
3. The law of justice.
4. The law of good faith and truthfulness.
5. The laws of mercy and forgiveness.

By mid-life, a person begins to know that, except for surface structures which change constantly, there really is nothing new under the sun. Younger persons do not recognize this because they have difficulty distinguishing the surface structures from the deep, changeless structure that is *humanity* (that part of us which reflects the image of our Creator). Only by mid-life or after do we learn that.

Prospero, in Shakespeare's *The Tempest,* keeps his daughter Miranda on an uninhabited island in order that she might never be cursed with the problems of civilization. When a shipwreck occurs on their coast, Miranda sees other humans for the first time.

"Oh, wonder!" she exclaims. "How many goodly creatures are there here! How beauteous mankind is! Oh, brave new world, that has such people in it!"

" 'Tis new to thee," answers her pessimistic father. He knows what these "goodly creatures" are capable of doing to his island paradise. He attempts in vain to protect Miranda from them.

I, too, would sometimes like to retreat to an island in the South Seas. I, too, would like to protect my family from the evils of civilization.

Whatever my fears, the younger generation will have to break its own illusion of how wonderful progress is. It will have to learn its own way of seeing below the structures that do change. The people of the next generation must learn for themselves what "building on sand" is all about before they care to work hard enough to get to the rock. " 'Tis new" to them.

No matter. The kingdom of God is forever and changes not. This is what forms our attitude toward society and shapes our lives within it. The fruits of the Spirit listed in Galatians 5:22-23—love, joy, peace, patience, kindness, goodness, faithfulness, gentleness, and self-control—are all very much "in" in God's society. As Christians, we must keep in mind that we live in two kingdoms simultaneously and that these two must often oppose one another—until "the kingdom of the world has become the kingdom of our Lord and of his Christ, and he will reign for ever and ever" (Rev. 11:15).

When the Israelites were about to take the Promised Land, the Lord commanded Joshua,

> Do not let this Book of the Law depart from your mouth; meditate on it day and night, so that you may be careful to do everything written in it. Then you will be prosperous and successful (Joshua 1:8).

People being people, it was not too long before

> another generation grew up, who knew neither the Lord nor what he had done for Israel. Then the Israelites did evil in

the eyes of the Lord and served the Baals. They forsook the Lord, the God of their fathers, who had brought them out of Egypt (Judg. 2:10-12a).

One of the saddest verses in the whole of Scripture appears at the very end of the book of Judges. It applies quite well to the do-your-own-thing culture of modern times: "In those days Israel had no king; everyone did as he saw fit" (Judg. 21:25).

People haven't changed much since then. As Solomon points out, "What has been done will be done again; there is nothing new under the sun" (Eccl. 1:9). People haven't changed much inside since Adam and Eve rebelled against the law of God, or since Cain slew Abel, or since the unbelief of Noah's neighbors, or since the immorality of Sodom. People are still sin filled.

God has not changed either. He loved people then; He loves them now. He demanded righteousness and obedience then; He demands it still. And by His Spirit, He empowers us now as then.

Living the Christian Attitude

I believe that there are few easy either/or answers to the tough ethical questions facing today's Christians. I also believe that your solutions to your problems will have to be individually applied according to God's Word. And I believe that "everyone who asks receives; he who seeks finds; and to him who knocks, the door will be opened" (Matt. 7:8). The reason that so many remain confused by these choices is that they do not *wish* to know the truth.

When the Jewish authorities were "confused" by the teachings of Jesus (though the common people understood Him well enough), Jesus told them, "Whoever is willing to do what God wants will know whether what I teach comes from God or whether I speak on My own authority" (John 7:17 TEV). That "still, small voice" will be there—*if you are listening*. And there is only one way to listen: open His Word to hear Him speak.

A great number of channels on my TV set and an even greater number of places on my radio dial vie for my attention, but I can listen to only one at a time. "There are all sorts of languages in the world, yet none of them is without meaning" (1 Cor. 14:10). But One has significance. Somewhere in your world, God has a voice. Are you tuned in?

14

Relating to the Same Old People

They have eyes, but they see nothing;
they have ears, but they hear nothing. . . .
    —Ezekiel (12:2b TEV)

You can be helped through mid-life crisis by relating to a new self and a new perspective of God. But once that's happened, how do you relate to the same ol' people around you?

For a while your crisis felt (or feels) like the old navy saying, "All men forward go aft; all men aft go forward; all men amidships stand by to direct traffic." You were (or are) in constant turmoil. Values are challenged; fashions and jobs changed; everything is up for grabs. Life is all questions and no answers. *So, how come no one else is upset?*

"I feel like Paul Revere, riding madly through the streets of Lexington, shouting, 'The British are coming!' " said Susan. "But nobody moves. It's not that they don't believe me; it's just that they don't see the significance of it."

Antoine de Saint-Exupéry, in his encounter with "the Little Prince," finds that he is persistently interrupted by the little fellow while trying unsuccessfully to fix his broken airplane, his only escape out of the desert where he is stranded. The Little Prince wants to talk about flowers.

> "Don't you see—I am very busy with matters of consequence!" [says Antoine].
>
> [The Little Prince] stared at me, thunderstruck. "Matters of consequence! . . . You talk just like the grown-ups! . . . I know a planet where there is a certain red-faced gentleman. He has never smelled a flower. He has never looked at a star. He has never loved anyone. He has never done anything in his life but add up figures. And all day long he says over and over, just like you: 'I am busy with matters of consequence!' " (*The Little Prince*, pp. 28-29)

I, too, find that while others around me are urgently discussing "matters of consequence," I want to talk about flowers. I *used* to be interested in "consequential matters," but lately, I'm not sure which matters will be found to have been consequential when I look back at them 10 years from now.

I'm not alone. Susan had the same problem. She was excited about new insights she had experienced. Her enthusiasm, however, was definitely *not* shared by her family and friends. They could not understand her new love of education, her plans to become gainfully employed, nor her subsequent lack of zealousness for laundry, vacuuming, or washing dishes. "I don't see what the problem is," she stated angrily. "All I ask for is a little cooperation so that I can get out two nights a week—and they act like I divorced them!

"Whenever I try to talk to them about anything that's important to *me*," she went on, "like my poetry class, or this therapy, or a book I read—they act like I'm from another planet. My Bible study group doesn't understand my contributions half the time, so I pretty much shut up or stay home—and then I'm accused of being lukewarm. No one seems to see things the way I do. Is there something wrong with me? Or is it with them?"

In *The Republic of Plato,* the philosopher is explaining to his brother Glaucon how difficult it is for those who have been "enlightened" to explain their state of enlightenment to those who are "unenlightened." Plato says, "Imagine the condition of men living in a sort of cavernous chamber underground . . . from childhood, chained by the leg and also by the neck, so that they cannot move and can see only what is in front of them, because the chains will not let them turn their heads."

The people in Plato's cave cannot see anything but the shadows cast on the wall by objects outside of the cave. They hear only echoes of the outside world. When they discuss with each other what they suppose to be the world, they discuss these shadows and echoes. In fact, they have prizes for those who have the keenest eye for the nuances of these shadows.

Suppose, says Plato, that a man should be set free from his chains. As he makes his way to the mouth of the cave, the light will temporarily blind him, and the unfamiliarity of the real objects would first confuse, then amaze, him. He is delighted with the new reality and attempts to go back to the cave and tell his friends about the real objects of which they have seen only shadows.

His friends, however, do not believe in the reality, having seen only the shadows. They laugh at him and say that he has gone mad, that he has gone to all that trouble to break the chains and leave the cave only to ruin his sight. "If they could lay hands on the man who was trying to set them free and lead them up, they would kill him," states Plato.

Don't Tell Anyone What Happened to You

Successfully surviving mid-life crisis with the help of God will "enlighten" you, but I caution you not to tell anyone. "Do not speak to a fool, for he will scorn the wisdom of your words," says Solomon (Prov. 23:9). Jesus echoes, "Do not give dogs what is sacred; do not throw your pearls to pigs. If you do, they may trample them under their feet, and then turn and tear you to pieces" (Matt. 7:6).

Here, then, is a precept:

It takes experiential knowledge to gain insight.

Once a person has "seen the light," he or she will understand some things that those in darkness will never learn by straining to read the shadows. St. Paul never learned Christ from books, though his own books were a great help to others. St. Paul learned Christ on the road to Damascus, falling to the earth on his knees in fear and humility.

Over and over again, the Bible tells of men and women who experienced God. It also tells of their friends who did not understand these people. Moses was railed at by the Israelites, from Egypt to the Promised Land. Jeremiah, Daniel, Isaiah— all were misunderstood. Jesus was killed.

We cannot *give* insight to others because we cannot give them the experience. For over 30 chapters, Job and his "comforters" (Eliphas, Bildad, Zophar, and Elihu) sit and analyze the workings of God, the sinfulness of humanity, and the problems between the two. They say some wise things and some foolish things. But Job is in the same state of mind as he began. What finally gave him insight?

My ears had heard of you
   but now my eyes have seen you.
Therefore I despise myself
   and repent in dust and ashes.

      — Job (42:5-6, italics mine)

We can tell all this to others, but they will not believe it until they have experienced it for themselves. Until then, it is all shadows.

I have seen it happen. Others will not accept as trivial those things that I have trivialized. There is, of course, the possibility that they are right and I am wrong. I think not; but then you never know. There is also the chance that, for them, the things are not trivial. If shadows are all they can see, they had better learn to see them well. The problems occur when we try to make each other see our truths in our ways.

A tremendous amount of research has been done by social psychologists on "locus of control." Persons with an *"external locus of control"* see events in their lives as being directed by those persons or forces around them. Those with an *"internal locus of control"* see their lives being directed by themselves.

Inner-directed persons take more responsibility for their lives. They are also happier, more cheerful, and exhibit fewer neurotic symptoms than do outer-directed persons.

The latter feel uncomfortable with new insights and seek to find refuge from them in two ways:

1. By feeling guilty for believing or feeling differently than others, and subsequently, by rejecting the new insight; or

2. By feeling hostile toward those who do not share their long-trusted understandings and thus insisting that others convert immediately (or face rejection).

You know you have *really* seen the light when it's okay with you that others enjoy their darkness. You have really experienced enlightenment when you no longer need to have others experience it in order to make you feel comfortable. Not that you don't care, but you know that *you* have changed for the better, no matter what they think. If and when they want to know why you are happier, you can tell them—but there's no point in shoving new insights down their throats. Doing so invites persecution. Jesus promised His disciples that if they follow Him, the world will hate them, persecute them, even kill them (John 15:18—16:3).

People are afraid of change. Confusion terrifies them. And if you remember back before your crisis, you were one of those people. Be patient with them. They're often like Lucille van Pelt (of "Peanuts" fame). When asked why she was ridiculing a certain political cartoon, she explained, "Because I don't understand it."

Have some understanding for the unenlightened. If they follow God in their own way, they will get the light that they need. If they do not, love them and pray for them. But do not attempt to convert those who do not wish to be converted.

On the other hand, do not let the unenlightened drag you down to the shadows. If you return to your former view of life, you will never be satisfied with it—or with yourself. You must be firm with them when they attempt to entice, coerce, or manipulate you into submission.

"But what do I do," asked Susan, "when they don't even *listen* to me before they start quoting Scripture, advising me to go and talk to the pastor, and giving me books on straying from sound doctrine? I feel sometimes like they must be right and *I* must be the one who's kooky. After all, *I'm* the one who changed."

St. Paul wasn't worried about other people's views. He tells the congregation at Corinth,

> I am not at all concerned about being judged by you or by any human standard; I don't even pass judgment on myself. My conscience is clear, but that does not prove that I am really innocent [of straying from God]. The Lord is the one who passes judgment on me (1 Cor. 4:3-4 TEV).

Sir Thomas More, in the movie *A Man for All Seasons,* is unconvinced that King Henry VIII is morally correct in divorcing his wife (I forget which) in order to marry another. More is coerced by his colleagues and the king himself—who laughs, scolds, and quotes Scripture. More is dismissed from his high court position and becomes poor. He is finally put into prison. After several months of enduring the bitter cold and the tremendous boredom of the tower, Sir Thomas is brought before a tribunal which has the power to hang him.

One of his old friends on the tribunal begs More to "come along with us, Thomas, for fellowship's sake."

"And when I go to hell for violating my faith," asks Sir Thomas (paraphrased), "will you also come along with *me* for fellowship's sake?" More is subsequently hanged.

I Simply Love the Same Ol' People

It seems to me that the question of how to relate to those who are unenlightened has been solved for us in Christ. He never seems to talk down to people. He was friendly, kind, and thoughtful. He praised where praise was due. In short, He loved those around Him—and they were hardly as enlightened as He was. After all, He was the Light.

On the other hand, you never see Jesus being pushed into doing anything He doesn't want to do, either. He responds negatively to coercion, whether from His family, His disciples, or the religious leaders.

Some of my clients who have taken assertiveness training ask me what they should be like as a result. "Be as assertive as Jesus was," is my answer. Philippians 2:5-8 sums it up quite nicely:

> Your attitude should be the same as that of Christ Jesus: Who, being in very nature God, did not consider equality with God something to be grasped, but made himself nothing, taking the very nature of a servant, being made in human likeness. And being found in appearance as a man, he humbled himself and became obedient to death—even death on a cross!

We should keep in mind always our own state of enlightenment. Compare it to *the* Light. Ours is dull, isn't it? Yet He consents, even delights, to love us.

If the brightness of an A can love all the way to the dullness of a Y, cannot the so-called brightness of the Y love the dullness of a Z?

We need to love as He has loved us; understand as He understands; forgive as He forgives. We need to relate to those same ol' people as He does.

God help us.

IV
The Conclusion of the Matter

He thought he saw an elephant
    That practiced on a fife:
He looked again, and found it was
    A letter from his wife.
"At length I realize," he said,
    "The bitterness of life!"

He thought he saw a Garden-Door
    That opened with a key:
He looked again, and found it was
    A Double Rule of Three:
"And all its mystery," he said,
    "Is clear as day to me."
        —*Lewis Carroll,* Sylvie and Bruno, *1889*

Hello. I must be going.
        —*Groucho Marx,* Animal Crackers

15

The Conclusion of the Matter

*Of making many books there is no end;
and much study wearies the body.*
          —Solomon (Eccl. 12:12)

When Solomon wrote the above, he didn't know the half of it. *Books in Print* lists well over 600,000 entries. The United States government prints almost 25,000 articles each year. There are over 30,000 newspapers and magazines printed each month. The file box of the Library of Congress lists over 73 million items. These all are the sum total of the wisdom of the last 5,000 years. That's not much though. Those 73 million items are expected to *double* in 10 or 15 years.

I cannot possibly hope to give you, in this short book, the entire knowledge and wisdom of all the ages (or even *this* age) on the subject of mid-living. I have quoted from a few dozen sources. If you would like a few hundred more, look in the reference sections of Jaques, Sheehy, Stevens-Long, Troll, and Yalom. They probably will lead you to two conclusions:

1. Solomon was right; much study wearies the body.
2. None of the books apply specifically to you.

William James, often cited as the father of modern psychology, believed passionately in the individuality of each person. He was fond of saying,

Probably a crab would be filled with a sense of personal outrage if it could hear us class it as a crustacean. "I am no such thing," it would say, "I am MYSELF, MYSELF alone."

This crisis of mid-life is happening not just to thousands of Americans and Europeans between the ages of 35 and 50. It is *happening to you!* (What's worse, it happened to me!)

No book can tell you how to cope with it adequately, for no book can consider *your* special personality, *your* unique circumstances, or *your* singular place in the kingdom of God.

Nevertheless, at the risk of missing your mark completely, I have attempted to share some pointers that were helpful to me and have been found helpful to others. In summary:

1. Stop trying to figure it all out.

Life (as the expression goes) is not meant to be a puzzle to be spent solving for the rest of your life. It is, rather, a *mystery for you to experience.* God has already given you enough answers in Jesus Christ, both to receive eternal life and to live now in a way that is pleasing to Him.

Shopenhauer, the great philosopher, spent his entire life in the endless pursuit of the meaning of life. At his life's end, he concluded that nothing matters; and since nothing matters, life is not worth living (paraphrased from *The Encyclopedia of Philosophy,* vol. 4). Solomon seems, at times, to give the same impression. But, if nothing matters, it should not matter to Solomon and Shopenhauer that nothing matters. Since both of them are very concerned *why* nothing matters, it follows that, for each of them, something actually does matter.

(If you didn't get that, reread the last sentence again. Or try this: If Mr. S worries about why x is worthless, then x must mean something to Mr. S, or he wouldn't worry about it. Clear?)

The pursuit of meaning, by itself, is fruitless. Meaning is a by-product of living. Therefore, forget to "pursue meaning." Instead, pursue life itself. Pursue God. And enjoy yourself under God.

Jack L. Chalker, in his science fiction thriller, *Exiles at the Well of Souls,* writes of a lost race called the Markovians. This extinct race had searched in vain for thousands of years for the meaning of life. When their utopian existence began to bore them, they transformed themselves into various lower races. One of those, the Gedenomdans, reinstituted the search.

> "We turned ourselves, not outward, but inward, to the very core of our being, our souls, if you will, and explored what we found there. . . . We're looking for what they [the Markovians] missed."
> "And have you found it?" [asks an inquirer].
> "After a million years, we are at the point where we perceive that something was indeed missing." (pp. 319—320)

There comes a time in the search for meaning, purpose, and God when one must rest upon faith. "There are some things that the Lord our God has kept secret; but He has revealed His law, and we . . . are to obey it forever" (Deut. 29:29 TEV).

2. Don't look back.

Learn from the past (by all means!), but don't dwell on it. The Lord counsels through Isaiah,

> Forget the former things; do not dwell on the past. See, I am doing a new thing! Now it springs up; do you not perceive it? I am making a way in the desert and streams in the wasteland (Is. 43:18-19).

I suppose that many Israelites missed the new thing that God did because they were focused on what God had done in the past through David and Solomon.

The "now" is the hardest thing to get anyone to stay with. We are so concerned about the past and the future that we miss what's happening now.

Sure, we would have been a much better parent/spouse/student or the like if we knew then what we know now. But we didn't. We were what we were. We did the best we could at the time. Let the past go. "No one who puts his hand to the plow and looks back is fit for service in the kingdom of God" (Luke 9:62). We fell short; we sinned; it is forgiven.

"Looking back" can take two forms. We either concentrate on how *wonderful* "the good old days" were and, subsequently, do nothing because "what's the use?"; or we concentrate on how *awful* things were and, subsequently, do nothing because "what's the use?"

Don't look back! "Banish anxiety from your heart and cast off the troubles of your body, for youth and vigor are meaningless" (Eccl. 11:10).

3. Enjoy yourself.

"I commend the enjoyment of life, because nothing is better for a man under the sun than to eat and drink and be glad. Then joy will accompany him in his work all the days of the life God has given him under the sun" (Eccl. 8:15).

C. S. Lewis, in his book *The Four Loves,* tells how the three "natural loves" (affection, friendship, and eros) are not enough on their own. They need to come under the control of agape—the love of God.

> To say this is not to belittle the natural loves but to indicate where their real glory lies. It is not disparagement to a garden to say that it will not fence and weed itself. . . . A garden is a good thing, but that is not the sort of goodness it has. (p.163)

In the same way, I stress that the "natural" remedies to the mid-life crisis (pleasure, family, and friendship) are not, *in themselves,* enough. This is not to say that they are evil. Long before God so loved this world enough to send His Son, God so loved the world enough to create it.

I am distressed by those who define their religion by what they are *not* allowed to do. The world is not my home, but it isn't a bad place to visit for "three score and ten" either.

If you ain't been dancing lately,
don't blame your shoes.
—Dr. Teeth and the Muppet Band, from TV's "The Muppet Show"

4. Improve yourself.

For heaven's sake (literally), get yourself unglued from the television (or whatever other trivial activity you pursue) and improve your body, mind, and spirit. Exercise; change your diet; read something you wouldn't ordinarily read; take a class; teach a class; read your Bible through cover to cover; ask your pastor to converse with you once a month about your spiritual condition. (It will improve his, too.)

Ask a psychologist to test you (this will cost money) to find out in what areas you need to grow; start having conversations with children—*real* conversations, not "how-old-are-you-what-grade-are-you-in?" Travel to a place you have never been or haven't seen in a long time; go to a marriage retreat or enrichment program; make your own retreat for one day with nothing but a notebook to write in; eat some ethnic food; learn sign language; play with a computer.

My wife's 90-year-old grandmother died recently. I remember picking her up for church and listening to her tell about the new exhibit at the museum and a book she was reading. At her funeral, people were heard to remark, "I never saw anyone so busy in my life; she sure didn't *act* 90."

It is possible to live only as long as life intoxicates us.
—Tolstoy, *My Confession*

5. Commit yourself to a cause.

Both Gail Sheehy and Irvin Yalom find in their research that membership in groups, commitment to some cause, and adoption of clear life goals are part of the "soul" of persons with high satisfaction and meaning in life. So is religion. This points to a happy condition for the Christian: Christ bids us, "Follow Me."

The trick is to avoid the busy work of "churchianity" and get to some kind of ministry that will be meaningful to you. Finding out what part of the body of Christ you are is never easy. There are all too many who will make you an "elbow" simply because they need an elbow. (Remember, though: one person's "busy work" is usually another person's meaningful ministry.)

Remember, also, that what was meaningful for you in your 20s may be useless and blowing after the wind for you in your

40s. For instance, at 25 I *loved* taking the church youth group on hayrides. Other persons my age still enjoy that, but I would rather work on a book now. However, at 25, you couldn't get me to write.

6. Involve yourself with others.

This may take some doing, especially for those of you who never got beyond the "Hi, how are you?" stage in church and at other places.

Listen to someone—your family, your friends, your brothers and sisters in Christ. Invite someone home for dinner whom you don't know very well. Join a club. Volunteer as a teacher's aide and listen to the kids (which very few people ever do).

Get the *Ungame* (or some other kinds of interaction-stimulating materials) at your local Christian bookstore. Use it with your family and your friends.

Ask your pastor if there are some shut-ins to visit.

Dare to be personal in your Bible study or Sunday school class. Share some things you've never shared before.

Read 1 John and ask yourself, "How can I put this into action?" Better yet, do it with some friends.

Fred brought Scotty into the Teen Challenge Center late one night. He had found the boy hitchhiking and zonked out on various kinds of drugs. He took Scotty home, sobered him up, fed and bathed him, and bought him new clothes.

For several weeks, Fred bailed Scotty out of trouble and literally kept him alive. Upon occasion, Scotty would attend church with Fred.

One night Scotty made a "decision for Christ." However, drugs and the street life remained a problem. So Fred convinced Scotty to join the Teen Challenge program. Scotty flunked out within a week, and Fred never saw him again.

Fred, however, was a changed man. Gone were the frequent migraine headaches and bouts with asthma. Gone was the almost constant depression, loneliness, and sense of meaninglessness. Fred began to make plans, upon his retirement from Ford Motor Company, to become a minister. "I don't know if the Lord did Scotty any good," Fred told me, "but He sure used that kid to change *my* life!"

7. Face the facts.

You *are* getting older. The world *is* changing, and there's not a thing you can do about it. You *are responsible* for having made the choices that made you the person you are and for making the choices that will determine the person you will become. *Death is drawing closer*; and unless God is real in Jesus Christ, you are all alone and without hope in this world.

These are not pleasant facts to face. But unless you consciously deal with them, they will control you. If you face them, you gain control over them.

Face the unpleasant, the secret sins, the unthinkable. Dive into the fears. Pour Light on the dark side of your soul (those childhood experiences that you tend to shrug off as over and done; the dreams that haunt; the fantasies that you admit to no one; the secret dream that never comes true; the tears and screams that you have held in check for so long). Then you will know the truth about yourself and be set free.

Jesus proclaimed the paradoxical truth that if you wish to save your life, you must first lose it; and if you wish to be strong, you must first be weak. If you wish to be spiritual, you must first see your carnality. If you want to be happy, pure, peaceful, and full of joy, you must first become intimate with pain, suffering, the filthy rags of your own righteousness. If you wish to become acquainted with the "butterfly of your spirit" (recalling de Saint-Exupéry's phrase), you must first make friends with the caterpillar of your soul.

There it is, theology fans: John's "Seven Simple Steps to Spiritual Success." Well, they *are* simple. All of God's truth is simple. "Follow Me; love your neighbors; leave that tree alone; bless those who curse you." All so simple.

But not so *easy*. When I attempt to cure a person of his fear of elevators by taking him for a 25-story ride and telling him to breath deeply and relax, it's *simple, but not easy*.

Paul compares the growing Christian to an athlete, a soldier, and a farmer (2 Tim. 2:3-6). These are demanding occupations. All demand discipline, energy, and a lot of time. All are painful, and all have risks involved. The farmer may work hard for little harvest. The athlete may come in second and never be recognized. The soldier may die. "Simple" jobs (at least in Paul's day), but hardly easy.

The mid-life transition takes about five years, according to most researchers. There are no shortcuts that I know of. Growing in Christ takes forever. You take whatever intellectual knowledge that you can find and apply it to the experiences that God allows to happen in your life. Mix well; pray without ceasing; and wait. And wait . . . and wait. And, behold! Out pops a new you!

Learn from Solomon

Solomon tried all the easy ways—great works, education, money, fame, and so forth. He drank himself silly, threw great parties, and impressed the queen of Sheba. He married far too many times, attempted to be religious, and ended up very depressed. I'm not sure if Solomon tried the hard way, though he surely wrote and lectured about it.

> Not only was the Teacher wise, but also he imparted knowledge to the people. He pondered and searched out and set in order many proverbs. The Teacher searched to find just the right words, and what he wrote was upright and true (Eccl. 12:9-10).

Even though Solomon became involved with other gods at the end of his life, his words remain true to our ears. At various "down" times of one's life, and especially at the time of mid-life evaluation, Ecclesiastes becomes powerful reading. Identifying with "the Teacher" can even be comforting, as one feels less alone in the dark. The comfort of these words, however, is well mixed with pain. It was meant to be.

> Now all has been heard; here is the conclusion of the matter: Fear God and keep his commandments, for this is the whole duty of man (Eccl. 12:13).

So much for the mid-life crisis. See you at old age.

References

Ackerman, Nathan, 1974. "The Family Approach to Marital Disorders." *Active Psychotherapy*. Edited by Harold Greenwald. New York: Jason Aronson, Inc.

Alexander, Lloyd, 1973. *The Foundling and Other Tales of Prydain*. New York: Holt, Rinehart and Winston, Inc.

Bonhoeffer, Dietrich, 1963. *The Cost of Discipleship*. New York: Macmillan Publishing Co., Inc.

Chalker, Jack, 1978. *Exiles at the Well of Souls*. New York: Ballantine Books, Inc.

Coleman, William, 1977. *The Pharisees' Guide to Total Holiness*. Minneapolis: Bethany House Publishers.

Conway, James, 1978. *Men in Mid-Life Crisis*. Elgin, IL: David C. Cook Publishing Co.

Cornford, Francis, 1945. *The Republic of Plato*. New York: Oxford University Press.

Detroit Free Press, Sunday, October 24, 1982, pp. 1b, 4b.

Draper, James, 1981. *Ecclesiastes: The Life Without God*. Wheaton, IL: Tyndale House Publishers.

Durant, Will, and Ariel Durant, 1968. *The Lessons of History*. New York: Simon & Schuster, Inc.

Fitzgerald, F. Scott, 1945. "Handle With Care." *The Crackup*. New York: J. Laughlin.

Flynn, 1974. *Mr. God, This Is Anna*. New York: Ballantine Books, Inc.

Fromm, Erich, 1956. *The Art of Loving*. New York: Bantam Books, Inc.

Heron House Editors, 1980. *The Odds: On Virtually Everything*. New York: Putnam Publishing Group.

James, William, 1958. *The Varieties of Religious Experience*. New York: New American Library.

Jaques, Elliot, October, 1965. "Death and the Mid-Life Crisis." *The International Journal of Psychoanalysis*.

Jung, Carl, 1960. "The Stages of Life." *The Collected Works of Carl Jung*. London: Routledge and Kegan Paul, Ltd.

143

Lair, Jess, 1972. *I Ain't Much Baby, But I'm All I Got.* Garden City, NY: Doubleday and Co., Inc.

Levinson, Daniel, 1978. *The Seasons of a Man's Life.* New York: Ballantine Books, Inc.

Lewis, Clive Staples, 1960. *The Four Loves.* New York: Harcourt, Brace, Jovanovich, Inc.

———, 1970. *The Lion, the Witch and the Wardrobe.* New York: Macmillan Publishing Co., Inc.

Mandell, Arnold, 1977. *The Coming of Middle Age.* New York: Summit Books.

Naisbitt, John, 1982. *Megatrends.* New York: Warner Books, Inc.

Newsweek, November 1, 1982. "Growing Old: Feeling Young," pp. 36—40.

———, November 1, 1982. "From Cars to Cocaine," pp. 56—58.

Phillips, J. B., 1961. *Your God Is Too Small.* New York: Macmillan Publishing Co., Inc.

Rosenfelt, Robert, 1965. "The Elderly Mystique." *The Journal of Social Issues.* 21, pp. 37—43.

Saint-Exupéry, Antoine de, 1943. *The Little Prince.* New York: Harcourt, Brace, Jovanovich, Inc.

Sheehy, Gail, 1976. *Passages.* New York: E. P. Dutton.

———, 1981. *Pathfinders.* New York: William Morrow and Co., Inc.

Stein, Joseph, 1970. "Fiddler on the Roof." *Best Plays of the Sixties.* Edited by S. Richards. Garden City, NY: Doubleday and Co., Inc.

Stevens-Long, Judeth, 1979. *Adult Life: Developmental Processes.* Palo Alto, CA: Mayfield Publishing Co.

Thompson, Ernest, 1979. *On Golden Pond.* New York: Dodd, Mead and Co.

Toffler, Alvin, 1970. *Future Shock.* New York: Random House, Inc.

Troll, Lillian, 1975. *Early and Middle Adulthood.* Monterey, CA: Brooks/Cole Publishing Co.

Whittaker, Carl, 1982. *From Psyche to System.* New York: The Guilford Press.

Williams, Mason, 1969. *The Mason Williams Reading Matter.* Garden City, NY: Doubleday and Co., Inc.

Wright, Norman, 1976. *An Answer to Depression.* Irvine, CA: Harvest House.

Yaconelli, Mike, 1976. *Tough Faith.* Elgin, IL: David C. Cook Publishing Co.

———, 1980. "The Back Door." *The Wittenberg Door.* December-January, p. 32.

Yalom, Irvin, 1980. *Existential Psychotherapy.* New York: Basic Books, Inc.